# Crime

What is the robbing of a bank compared to
the founding of a bank?
*Bertholt Brecht*

# Crime

Five Leaves Publications
www.fiveleaves.co.uk

**Crime**
Edited by Ross Bradshaw

Published in 2013
by Five Leaves Publications,
PO Box 8687, Nottingham NG1 9AW
www.fiveleaves.co.uk

ISBN: 978 1 907869 79 2

Collection copyright
© Five Leaves Publications

Copyright for individual essays
rests with the contributors

Five Leaves acknowledges support
from Arts Council England

Typeset and designed by Five Leaves
and Four Sheets Design and Print
Printed in Exeter by Imprint Digital

it might be pleasant to live on the edge of the Lake District: walking in the hills every weekend, cycling round Coniston, being close to nature. I'd been brought up to value the hills. My grandfather's brother, Bruce Clucas, was a poor man's Wainwright who once encountered the editor of the *Lancashire Evening Post* on top of a peak and challenged him to publish guides to local walks. Over twenty years or so, great-uncle Bruce's routes appeared weekly and were collected into little volumes, *Thirty Rambles*, *Forty Rambles*, which sold like Kendal Mint Cake to the working classes who wanted to escape the factories, the smoke, the terraced streets, the noise, the rowdy pubs, the vulgarity of industrial towns like Preston where he lived and worked. He started as a part-timer in Horrockses Mill at the age of 12 and retired at 65. He was a typical working-class autodidact and had a neat little library of several hundred serious books. Into his 90s he was still signing up for weekend courses on *Love In The Novels of Thomas Hardy* or *The Industrial Revolution in Lancashire*. The walking doesn't seem to have done him any harm: he lived to be 99.

My interview coincided with the Windscale inquiry of 1977 which took place in Whitehaven Civic Hall. BNFL wanted to establish an oxide fuel reprocessing plant (THORP) at the Windscale facility and seemed to be facing little opposition until an article in the *Daily Mirror* in October 1975 got public disquiet simmering. Peter Shore, Secretary of State for the Environment set up the inquiry and appointed Mr Justice Roger Parker to head it. It ran from June to November 1977 and granted BNFL everything they asked. Shore, very cleverly rejected the BNFL application for full acceptance of the report which was published in March 1978 and invited parliament to debate it, thereby granting the company putative democratic authority. Sellafield, as it is today, employs many in Whitehaven. Derrick Bird worked there as a joiner till he was sacked for minor theft in 1990. He was in his early thirties at the time. His father was still alive. He was still

# One Day in Whitehaven
## *Alan Dent*


If you don't come from Cumbria, or perhaps the northwest, though you may have visited the Lake District you probably won't have been to Whitehaven. It tries hard these days to be a tourist destination: it's one of only two "gem towns" in Cumbria, the other being Cockermouth, famous for Wordsworth and the terrible floods of 19th November 2009 when the Derwent and the Cocker broke their banks. Whitehaven's right-angled, grid-plan of streets is thought to have been the model for New York; John Paul Jones attacked it in 1778; Washington's grandmother, Mildred Gale, was born there; it boasts some of the finest Georgian buildings in the country; it has hosted a maritime festival in its harbour since 1999. But it's outside the Lake District and it's urban. In Grasmere or Ambleside, strolling up Catbells or pushing hard up Stickle Ghyll, riding the pleasure boat on Windermere or sitting in a teashop in Hawkshead, you can pretend the urban world is remote; you can act out, gently of course, the fantasy that this is the real England; a rural place, a quiet place, a place of healthy pursuits, fresh air, hardiness and heartiness. You can forget there are such things as ASBOs and you can get nostalgic for the comforting beauty of nature. At the time of the July 1981 riots in Moss Side and Toxteth, Willie Whitelaw, interviewed in his home in Penrith, just an hour's drive north of Whitehaven, said that when he saw the events on television he wondered what was happening to England, but then he looked out of his window and surveyed the acres of his beautiful estate and knew that was the real England. Cumbria is a place of fantasy, as its best writers know.

When I qualified as a teacher in 1977 my first job interview was at Whitehaven High School. I naively imagined referred to was in fact his brother. "If this is indeed a mistake I am sorry for the inconvenience," his short email concluded; "but I would like to know as would my brother and my mother as we don't know what happened to him for all these years." I was able to put him in contact with the Coroner's office, who were apparently able to confirm that the Michael Stansfield in the article was indeed his brother. Not a happy ending as such, but an ending all the same.

Since this article was first published, Dr Chapman has retired. The Coroner's Court has relocated to the Council House on Old Market Square.

avoidable death? "No," he said, briskly. "No. This is a job. You can feel tremendous sympathy for the family, and express it in court, but you can't let it get to you. You can't."

There were no camera crews on the courthouse steps for Michael Stansfield's inquest, held on 24 April 2009, three weeks after his death. There were no family members leaning forward in their seats; no family or friends at all. Instead, it was attended by the housing association staff who had found his body, the detective who led the police investigation and a journalist from the *Nottingham Evening Post*. The proceedings were brief. Chapman outlined the report of the post-mortem examination, which had found death was caused by a heroin overdose. The housing association staff described the circumstances in which they found his body, and what little they knew about him: he had suffered from mental health problems for a long time and was due to see a doctor on the day he died. The detective described the findings at the scene, concluding that no one else had been involved and there was no indication of suicide.

After summarising the evidence, Chapman asked the journalist to publish an appeal for any of Stansfield's family members to come forward. "Otherwise," he said, "we'll just have to see what we can do for him ourselves." He returned a verdict of accidental death, and left the court to begin making arrangements for the funeral.

## Post-script

Around six months after this piece was first published in the *Guardian Weekend* magazine, I received an email from a Jonathan Stansfield, asking for further details on the Michael Stansfield referred to in the piece. He explained that no-one in his family had seen or heard from Michael for seventeen years, and that as the ages appeared to correlate he was keen to find out if the man the mistakes she had made: "That was an error of judgement," she said more than once. "I have since altered my practice." (Chapman commented on this later, saying it had made the whole inquest easier for everyone and was one of the few positive aspects of the case. "The ones you have to worry about are the doctors who sit there and refuse to accept they've done anything wrong. They're the ones who aren't going to learn from their mistakes.")

Towards the end of the hearing, a consultant paediatric kidney specialist was called to give evidence, and asked a simple question: would Bethany have survived had she had a blood test soon after her first appointment? "Absolutely," he said with a devastating lack of hesitation. The family's solicitor pressed the point: what was the latest opportunity at which Bethany's life could have been saved? "Accepting that she may have required dialysis and a kidney transplant," he said, "I would say her life could have been saved up to about two or three days before her death." There was a long, winded silence in the court.

The next day, Chapman showed me the press reports. He'd returned a narrative verdict, an option that leaves the coroner free to declare exactly how the death occurred, and had kept it as brief as possible so that it would be quoted in full: Bethany's death, he'd said, "was caused by a natural disease which was both preventable and treatable". This was intended to highlight the failures and omissions that had preceded her death, but in many of the press reports his verdict had been abbreviated to the almost meaningless "caused by a natural disease". He consoled himself with the comments made by the family's solicitor that they were "grateful... that the circumstances surrounding her death have been made public".

I wondered whether cases such as this ever affected him or his staff emotionally. Obviously they must get used to dealing with sudden and tragic deaths, and develop a distance, but with a young child and such an each, I would hope, is treated with sincerity and the dignity it deserves."

He started to gather up his files, then turned back to me. "I can quote you one. With suicide, you have to be satisfied that someone intended to die. It's not just the act; they have to intend to die. And there was a case with a very old lady who took some pills, and she was quite confused, and I thought she'd taken them because she was confused. But then I had a letter from her husband, years later, which said, 'I have committed suicide. Don't mess up my inquest like you did my wife's.' So, you know, you can't always win."

Every case might be important to somebody, as Chapman says, but only some cases are deemed important enough to bring camera crews to the courthouse steps, and to fill the court with journalists and solicitors, and be reported in the national press. Bethany Townsend's inquest, held the day after Victoria Brealey's, was one of those.

Bethany was six when she died, suffering from acute chronic kidney failure and other complications, on 22 January 2007. Her father, teacher and GP were called to give evidence as the court pieced together the narrative of her last weeks: a series of oversights, administrative failings and errors of judgement that meant a girl weighing just 15kg at the time of her first appointment with the GP — when she was reported as drinking excessively, bedwetting, not eating and being lethargic — wasn't referred to a specialist until three and a half weeks later; a referral of which her father was informed, by awful coincidence, on the evening she died.

The GP, who had failed to ensure a blood test was taken and an urgent referral made, and had kept Bethany's urine sample in a fridge over the weekend instead of sending it straight to the lab, was the focus of sustained questioning at the hearing. But there was something quietly impressive about the way she faced up to her responsibilities in the courtroom and acknowledged the weekend — deaths in a care home, in a public park, in hospital, a young man found by his parents at home — and making notes for his staff to follow up. This was a quiet Monday, as spring Mondays usually are. In winter there can be fifty reports coming in over a weekend, rising to 150 after the Christmas break. "Occasionally," he had told me earlier, "I get a new financial wizard in the council who writes and says, 'We're going to knock 15% off your budget next year.' And I write back and say, 'Thank you very much. Will you tell 15% of the local population not to die?' "

Chapman's reputation locally, particularly among medical professionals, is rather stern; he sees his duty, in part, as uncovering their mistakes. ("When it comes to record-keeping," he said, "as far as I'm concerned, if they haven't written it, they haven't done it.") He is clearly conscious of his image as a public office-holder: he makes a point of wearing his wig and gown to civic events, and is careful to avoid anything that could bring the office into disrepute ("I drive very slowly; I don't drink"). And he has been known to open the talks he gives about his work by fixing the audience with a grim stare and announcing, "Every dead body in Nottinghamshire belongs to me."

I spoke to Chapman on a number of occasions during the week I was there, usually in the office while he was also dealing with telephone inquiries from pathologists, police officers and members of the public, or signing documents, or advising officers and administrators dealing with awkward situations. And though he was scrupulous about never discussing ongoing cases ("Everything out there is public," he said, pointing towards the courtroom, "everything in here is not"), I wondered whether there might be any past cases he was able to discuss — were any particularly memorable?

He thought for a moment. "Every case is important to somebody, therefore it's important to me. Clearly, some cases are easier than others, some more memorable. But were not entirely unrelated, he added, ruling out a verdict of natural causes. "We simply do not and cannot know exactly what led to this death," he said, using a phrase I was to hear him repeat throughout the week I attended his inquests. It seemed an obvious truth, and one that left the family little comfort. He returned an open verdict, and offered his deepest condolences.

The Brealeys left the court and went to the café across the road. "We were quite deflated," Beverley said. "We just sat there looking at each other. We weren't sure what had gone off. It was shorter than we'd expected, and traumatic, having to relive the whole thing again. Dr Chapman was very fair, he did a good job, asked good questions and really put one of the doctors in knots. But I wanted answers and solutions, and I didn't get them."

The family's solicitor has advised them not to pursue a legal case, for lack of evidence, but Beverley is still writing to the hospital, still hoping for an acknowledgement that something went wrong, an apology. "I don't think open verdicts help families," she said. "I think the coroner needs to pursue it further until he gets a proper verdict. Somebody's got to be at fault, haven't they?"

Dr Chapman has been the coroner for Nottingham since 1993. A briskly spoken man in his late 50s, with a headmasterish air, he gives the impression of being at pains to conceal both a deep compassion and the pride he feels in his work. One of the first things he told me was that coroners are not allowed to apportion blame. "People still sometimes come with a lot of expectations. They think that, like the big lottery finger, I'm going to point to somebody and say, 'It's your fault.' That's not my role. My role is to hear all the facts. If you want to blame somebody, there are other courts in which to do it." It's something families can find hard to accept, he said.

We were sitting by the window of his large, open-plan office, looking out at commuters emerging from the station. It was 7.30 on a Monday morning and Chapman was glancing through the reports that had come in over treatment for bone cancer, had died from perforations to her bowel within hours of being given a sigmoidoscopy (an internal examination of the bowel). The witnesses, guided by Chapman, went through the medical history, referring to thick folders of notes and occasionally looking up at the family. It became clear that the possibility of a connection between the sigmoidoscopy and Mrs Brealey's death was the underlying focus of all the questions, and the reason the family were leaning forward so intently, folding their arms and shaking their heads and tutting every now and again. The coroner kept coming back to this point, taking care to ensure the discussion could be readily understood by the family. ("When you say the larger perforation was 'in the transverse colon' — that's right round the bend, isn't it?") Was Mrs Brealey in pain after her examination, he asked. Could her cancer treatment have affected her bowels? Why was there such a delay between her first report of abdominal pains and her diagnosis? And could the registrar explain, he asked, in a dramatic crescendo that prompted gasps from the family, why one of the times in Mrs Brealey's medical notes had been altered?

But the witnesses from the hospital were also encouraged to detail the extent of Mrs Brealey's illness, and the steps they had taken to treat her. At one point, the family's solicitor asked why she had become so ill when she had been diagnosed with "mild myeloma". On the contrary, her doctor said, the diagnosis was "multiple myeloma". She was in serious pain; her illness was not responding to treatment, her prognosis was not good. He turned to the family and gently emphasised the point: "Mrs Brealey did not have a mild illness."

After two hours, Chapman moved to his summing up. He commented on the delays in treatment and diagnosis between Mrs Brealey's examination and her death. He noted that the larger of the two bowel perforations had occurred naturally, making a verdict of accidental death impossible. But the internal examination and its aftermath

The family were kept informed while they waited for the inquest; they were given the results of the post-mortem examination and were able to ask questions about the investigation. They were offered the opportunity to visit the court before the hearing, so they would know what to expect, but Beverley's father didn't feel able to face it.

On the day, the family arrived early and were shown into a side room. "That was a bit daunting," Beverley said. "It felt like we were being kept out of the way of the witnesses." What had she thought the court was going to look like? "I don't know. I thought it was going to be a proper court, like you see on television. But it wasn't. It was just a room."

The courtroom is long and narrow and simply furnished: a dozen short rows of soft chairs, a table for the witnesses, a desk for the press and a raised bench for the coroner. There are jugs of water on the coroner's bench and press desk, and a box of tissues on the witness table. Tall windows look out over a busy road which runs past the station; in the hushed minutes before an inquest, the noise from the street — music, shouting, buses starting and stopping — can be so intrusive that the windows have to be kept closed on even the warmest days.

I watched as the clerk showed people to their seats: a journalist from the local paper, two solicitors with wheeled cases full of files, half a dozen doctors and other hospital representatives, and, finally, the Brealeys, a dozen strong, squeezing into the front three rows. They sat, and whispered, and shuffled through their papers. They shifted in their chairs. The clock moved slowly towards 10.

The clerk told everyone to stand and the coroner for Nottingham, Dr Nigel Chapman, walked in, took his seat at the bench, and opened the inquest. One by one, the doctors were called to the witness table. There was no attempt to explain the background to the case — everyone there knew what had happened — but gradually the story emerged: Mrs Brealey, who had been receiving gathered, evidence collected and a date for an inquest hearing set.

I first visited Nottingham coroner's court in 2008, as research for a novel I was working on. The administrator asked which inquest I wanted to attend. "It depends what you're interested in," he said, turning the pages of a large desk diary. "We've got a road traffic and an industrial tomorrow morning, a hanging in the afternoon. On Wednesday we've got a baby and another road traffic. Thursday's quiet." As an introduction to the dailiness of sudden death, this was hard to beat.

I was fascinated, then, by the work being done in the coroner's office, on the public's behalf but almost entirely out of the public eye; the bureaucratic ritual with which quiet lives and ordinary deaths were being held up to the light of scrutiny and entered into the records of the state. It felt strange that an institution with such a long history, and a key role in civil society, would have such a low public profile. I was intrigued by the stories I'd glimpsed on that first visit, so last April, with the novel finished, I went back to learn more.

When Beverley Brealey's mother, Victoria, died, on 8 May 2008, it was almost a year before the inquest was held. "All that time waiting just delayed our grieving process," Beverley said. "We couldn't move on without getting some answers about what had happened in that hospital."

Victoria Brealey was 62 when she died, in the Nottingham hospital where she was being treated for bone cancer. Her death was sudden, and followed what had seemed a routine procedure; the family immediately felt that something had gone wrong, that, as Beverley puts it, "she wasn't meant to die". Within hours, Beverley had been contacted by the coroner's office to say they were in receipt of her mother's body and were ordering a post-mortem examination. She was pleased, she said: she didn't feel the hospital was giving her family the answers they were looking for.

# Inside the Coroner's Court
## *Jon McGregor*

*Close to half of all deaths in England and Wales are sudden, unnatural or unexplained, and referred to a coroner's court. So why do we know so little about what goes on there?*

Michael Stansfield was lying on a sofa in the hallway of his flat when they found his body. He was still warm, but he wasn't breathing. The housing association staff who had come looking for him called the ambulance, and the police, and when the ambulance arrived Stansfield was declared dead at the scene. It was 1 April 2009. He was 43. The police examined the scene and found evidence of heroin use; the staff confirmed that Stansfield was known to have used drugs. There was no record of next of kin, so none was contacted. His body was taken away to the hospital mortuary and the coroner was informed.

In England and Wales, the coroner must be informed of any death within his or her jurisdiction that is sudden, unnatural, unexplained, or for which a doctor has been unable to certify the cause. Approaching half of all deaths fit these criteria: the Nottingham coroner's court, one of the busiest in the country, opens inquiries into around 6,000 deaths a year. In most cases, those will be limited to contacting the dead person's GP, discussing medical history and allowing a death certificate to be issued; if the GP is unable to give a cause of death, or if there is any uncertainty about the circumstances, the coroner can order a post-mortem examination, and will often be able to issue a death certificate without further inquiry. But if the death is not found to be from natural causes, or if there is remaining uncertainty about the circumstances, an inquest will be formally opened, witness statements

In this collection we explore different aspects of crime. We start off with reportage, essays on "true crime" and end with crime fiction.

Our previous volumes were *Maps* and *Utopia*, as mentioned. Next year it will be *Rock* (that's the music, not geology) and in 2015 we'll explore *London*.

*Ross Bradshaw*
Five Leaves
September 2013

# Introduction

Welcome to Five Leaves' annual volume of themed essays. The last edition was *Utopia*. *Crime* is perhaps a counterpoint.

We are, most of us, partners in an unwritten social contract, as Rousseau and others suggested. We work if we can, we bring up our children to respect others, we pay our taxes because we want to support those in need and if we are in need we have a right to expect those around us to provide a safety net. Some on the Conservative/Republican right would prefer otherwise and companies like Starbucks, Amazon and the Arcadia Group see no need to pay taxes. The rest of us have worse and fewer public services because of corporate tax avoidance, but are also daily confronted by those others who do not fulfil their side of the social contract where we agree that it is better to avoid robbing our neighbours and would rather they did not throw bricks at us over the garden fence.

Yet most of us read and enjoy crime fiction, and accept that there are times when it is necessary to break the law. Nobody says that Rosa Parks should have written a polite letter to her Member of Congress requesting the right to sit at the front of the bus. Nobody says that Gandhi might have really been better off had he gone through the proper channels. Some readers here might have refused their poll tax demands, engaged in gay relationships before they were legal or would, at least in theory, support those who, in extremis, have engaged in mercy killing. Certainly I did not think I was a criminal when I was fined one pound in 1970 in Glasgow for illegally flyposting about the Vietnam War, nor, later, on frosty mid-winter sit-downs at nuclear bases. Some laws are there to be broken.

| | |
|---|---|
| **Junior Crime Reporter**<br>*Peter Mortimer* | 116 |
| **Dando the Oyster-Eater:**<br>**The Life and Times of a Bouncing, Seedy Swell**<br>**on a Bilking Spree**<br>*Ann Featherstone* | 120 |
| **"I Loved Charlie":**<br>**The Amazing Criminal Exploits and**<br>**Astounding Cultural Afterlife of the Great**<br>**Portico Thief Charles Peace**<br>*Michael Eaton* | 128 |
| **The Dark Eyes of London**<br>Cathi Unsworth | 141 |
| **Lines of Enquiry**<br>John Harvey | 173 |
| **Marlow and Me**<br>Russel D McLean | 186 |
| **What You Don't Know about Nottingham**<br>*David Belbin* | 196 |
| **Waking the Silent Suspect**<br>*Hilary Spiers* | 206 |
| **Acknowledgments** | 209 |
| **Contributors' Notes** | 212 |

# Contents

| | |
|---|---:|
| **Introduction**<br>*Ross Bradshaw* | 7 |
| **Inside the Coroner's Court**<br>*Jon McGregor* | 9 |
| **One Day in Whitehaven**<br>*Alan Dent* | 19 |
| **The Love Killers: Thoughts on Dyadic Death**<br>*Rod Madocks* | 32 |
| **Riders on the Storm**<br>*Melanie McGrath* | 50 |
| **Knuckling Under:**<br>**The Politics of Police Work in Weimar Berlin**<br>*Damien Seaman* | 63 |
| **The First Murderer**<br>*John Lucas* | 73 |
| **Portland**<br>*Paul Barker* | 85 |
| **Scrappin' wi' Scouse**<br>*John Stuart Clark* | 88 |
| **Convicted Out of his Own Mouth?**<br>**How Forensic Linguistics Cleared Derek**<br>**Bentley's Name**<br>*Danuta Reah* | 100 |
| **The Kerry Babies Case: a Crime Against Women**<br>*Deirdre O'Byrne* | 107 |

married to Linda. There were no disputes over wills. Theft from workplaces is of course common. People tend not to see it as theft. But when you work in a nuclear installation taking things home is a bit different from dropping a few pens in your handbag or shoving half a ream of paper up your jumper. The people of West Cumbria depend on an industry mocked in Cumbrian novelist John Murray's masterpiece *Radio Activity* as "the biggest liar in the world". Murray once lived in Cleator Moor, just a few miles from Whitehaven. One of his friends is the writer Frederick Lightfoot whose parents were the publicans of *The Hound Inn*, Frizington where ordinary bloke Derrick Bird used to drink. Now in the north of the county, in Brampton, close to the Debatable Lands he loves so much, Murray is the author of eight novels and a collection of stories, *Pleasure*, which won the Dylan Thomas award in 1988. He co-edited the fiction magazine *Panurge* with David Almond, the children's writer whose *Skellig* was a great success. Apart from his time at Oxford where he studied Sanskrit and a brief spell in London, Murray has lived all his life in Cumbria. His novels are set there. He knows its many accents inside out. He dislikes the Lake District, stays away from Carlisle, has little affinity with the West Cumbria where he grew up but loves Brampton and north Cumbria. His novels imaginatively render the life of this big, remote county and its odd characters and connect it to the world at large. In his latest, *The Legend of Liz and Joe*, Joe Gladstone runs a guest house whose would-be occupants have to write an essay to gain admittance, Joe not wishing to cater to the dull or ignorant. On its first page is the line "...and be assured that some of those slavering countrymen will only be happy when they have potshotted more or less everything that moves." This is in response to an hysterical letter in the local media about the scourge of grey squirrels. The narrator recalls when the reds were just as sought after. In Cumbria, shooting is a solution.

If you think Cumbria is a quiet, twee place populated by gentle, uncomplicated souls remote from the corruptions and machinations of the city, read Murray's novels. Their hilarious plots are complemented by lunatic or near-lunatic characters. Nowhere will you find the tourist board image of good folk in boots and anoraks heading off for a healthy day on the fells or replenishing their energy with a cream tea as the sun sets behind Skiddaw. Cumbria, like everywhere is a real place and a locale of the mind.

The events of 2nd June brought the two into collision. How could such things happen in a peaceful, rural county? How could such things be done by an ordinary bloke?

I took the train from Preston the day before my interview in 1977. I remember feeling pleased I'd found a job to apply for in such a nice place, though I'd never been to Whitehaven. The Lake District I knew quite well. My first holiday independent of my family was at the age of fourteen in 1965 when Pete Southworth and I packed our saddlebags and cycled up to Ambleside for a week's youth hostelling. We covered sixty or seventy miles on our first day, but after that the distances declined dramatically. We met other teenagers and did what teenagers like to do: we hung out. We were all supposed to be walking or cycling, but the attraction of wasting hours doing nothing but being together and talking ( about nothing) was far stronger than the desire to conquer peaks or clock up miles. Most of us were urban: Preston, Birmingham, Chester-le-Street, Newcastle-under-Lyme, Leeds; we exchanged stories about the places we lived. It was exciting to know young people all over the country were doing the same things, part of the same culture; much more exciting than tea shops and cagoules. And there were girls. This was the first time I'd been away from the admonition of parents and teachers in mixed company. The possibility of a snog was ever-present. But it didn't happen. I remember well one of the lads we met. A few years older than us, he was a fan of Billy J. Kramer and the Dakotas and modelled the quiff he was endlessly combing on his hero. He sang Kramer's songs all the time too and though he never said so, obviously imagined himself a future pop star. I'd never met anyone who so obviously acted out the fantasy that was in millions of young heads. I didn't like him. I found him vain, cynical and arrogant. But he got to snog the girls.

Two years later I went to the Lakes for a walking holiday with my mates Pete Nightingale and Ian Carter. We went swimming in Rydal Water and when I came out, numb with cold, I found I'd gashed my foot. A girl at the youth hostel who was training to be a nurse in Sunderland patched me up. We sat on the grass in the grounds and she cleaned the wound with antiseptic before putting on butterfly bandages. She told me it really needed stitches and I should have had a tetanus jab. She was older than me and very calm and sweet. I fell in love with her for the afternoon because she was pretty and kind. But I didn't get to snog her. We drank underage pints in the Salutation in Ambleside and stumbled back to the dorm feeling very grown up. Couples disappeared from the hostel common-room into the night and there was talk of heavy petting. My boots didn't get muddy.

Nevertheless, sitting in the rocking carriage as it made its way north, I was still prey to the myth of the Lake District idyll. I was travelling in the direction of simplicity and authenticity, away from the dirty urban, the rush, the noise, the posturing, the pub fights, the racism, the football hooligans, the high-rise flats and small-town small-mindedness. I was heading for Wordsworth's country. When Wordsworth was told the Lakes couldn't match the Alps he said: "Don't confuse sublimity with magnitude." I was bound for sublimity. I'd booked into a little hotel and the first person I met after checking in was a young scientist giving evidence to the Windscale inquiry. He was absolutely opposed to

THORP. He considered the inquiry a joke. He made me feel very ignorant because I didn't understand the science and hadn't kept abreast of the inquiry. I had a drink with him in the hotel bar and then went to explore the town. Talking to him had made me slightly gloomy, or at least dispelled the mood of the train journey. Here I was in Whitehaven and what was going on? According to the young scientist a whitewash and a stitch-up to let the powerful interests of BNFL prevail. Some sublimity.

What did I expect to find in Whitehaven? There are some places which though small are intriguing, but I walked from one end to the other in minutes and found nothing to make me feel it had that quality. Exploring every street in the town centre took no time at all. Just about everything was shut. Few people were about. This was small, small town and I quickly got the feeling it wasn't the kind of place where there were disparate communities and the possibility of getting to know a like-minded circle. By the time I'd walked round for an hour and had a half in an empty pub, I was pretty sure it wasn't for me. There were clear signs of economic decline and none of imagination. Those silly sentiments I'd had on the train evaporated. I went back to my hotel room knowing if I was offered the job the next day, I'd have to turn it down. There were four of us for interview, one was a garrulous young woman who had been educated in the school and felt she was the front-runner. I liked the place. It had a very good feel: serious yet relaxed. The pupils were well-behaved and polite and you could tell from their faces and demeanour they were a pretty happy lot. The Headteacher was pleasant too: the interview was informal. I kept wondering when the chat was going to end and the interview proper begin. And then it was over. They offered me the job and were disappointed when I had to say no. I explained why: I didn't think I could live in Whitehaven. I'd thought being close to the Lakes would appeal to me, but the town was a place I couldn't belong. I was sorry, but I didn't think I'd be happy there.

In those days, you got expenses for attending interviews, otherwise I'd've rung early and said I was withdrawing. On the train home I thought about looking for jobs in Manchester or London. When I walked out of the station, Preston seemed a metropolis in comparison to Whitehaven.

Close-knit communities: one of the many clichés that have informed the reporting of the events of June 2nd in West Cumbria. The assumption is that in such communities people find support and comfort. You don't expect, therefore, men to pick up guns and go on the rampage in a close-knit community. In what kind of community then would you expect such behaviour? A loose-knit one? One week after the carnage the Rector of Whitehaven described the violence as "inexplicable". Inexplicability and bewilderment have characterised the reaction, not only of the media, but of the local population, and perhaps the country as a whole. Is this because, if a man had killed twelve people in an hour in Moss Side, Manchester or Bootle or Brixton, if someone had run amok on the Blackbird Lees estate in Oxford, then everyone would have found that explicable: poverty, drugs, alienation, violence. I've just watched a BBC news report about the tributes paid in West Cumbria today, 9th June, one week on, and it began with a reference to "rolling hills" and the "Old England". Do hills stop people being violent? Is massacre something new? What kind of world did Derrick Bird belong to? What kind of culture shaped his mind? Much has been made of the fact he'd lived all his fifty-two years in West Cumbria; this in a society which prides itself on social mobility. The sentimentality of course, like mine on the train in 1977, is that he wanted to stay because he belonged, because the community was close-knit, because Cumbria is a place folk don't want to leave. Perhaps. But maybe it's also a place they can't escape. Derrick Bird's father, Joe, was a manual worker. Derrick left education early. What were his chances of ever breaking away from this place where everyone knew everyone else's business, where there was no space to be anonymous? The city provides relief. You can always go somewhere where people don't know you; they don't know your twin brother is much more successful or that you've a record for petty crime; you can walk among strangers. But in a close-knit community almost everyone knows everyone. All the same, Derrick Bird had his secrets. He didn't go to Thailand just for the scuba-diving but his use of prostitutes and his falling for one of them and sending her substantial sums of money weren't the things that made people testify to what a nice, ordinary bloke he was. If Derrick Bird was an ordinary bloke, we are in very serious trouble.

Glenda Pears, manager of L&G Taxis in Whitehaven said Bird was "a real nice man." Councillor John Kane said he was "very placid…very quiet" and "kept himself to himself." Sue Matthews, a telephonist at A2B Taxis said he was a "quiet fellow". Peter Leder who spent the evening of Tuesday 1st June with him and to whom Bird said on leaving: "You won't see me again", judged him "an outgoing well-known guy, who everyone liked." His next door neighbour but one, Ryan Dempsey, thought him "very approachable". Michelle Haigh of The Hound Inn described him as "a normal bloke". It was said of him he liked "tinkering" with cars. Tinkering is just right : harmless, aimless, easy-going. This was how Derrick Bird was viewed. In his close-knit community where people are supposed to know one another so well, among the rolling hills of Old England, this man who harboured murderous thoughts for years was universally judged to be an innocuous, good chap. On the evening of Tuesday 1st June he argued with fellow cab drivers. It was petty stuff but afterwards he shook all their hands and said: "There's going to be a rampage tomorrow." It was well known he owned guns.

The night before a man goes berserk and kills twelve people he says there will be a rampage and no-one responds. He tells a friend he won't see him again and the friend does nothing. This is remote, quiet, peaceful Cumbria, a cockstride from the pretty teashops and homely pubs beloved of walkers; a place where barristers, journalists, consultants and headteachers have second homes. This is Old England. This is a place of close-knit communities. People don't flip and commit mass murder in a place like this. Oh yes they do. What's more, they tell people they're going to do it. When a man leaves a friend in the early hours and says he won't see him again, isn't he trying to alert him? Isn't he calling for help? When he formally shakes hands with all his colleagues and tells them tomorrow he's going on the rampage, isn't he asking to be listened to? How come people in close-knit communities in Old England don't know how to read these signs? Why didn't someone ask him what he meant? Why didn't someone report his disturbing comment to the police? Why didn't someone put two and two together and see this was a man in a desperate state, a man about to tip over the edge?

The myth that has generated such puzzlement and disbelief is that there are parts of Britain (Old England, the rolling hills, close-knit communities, Willie Whitelaw's real England) where contemporary culture doesn't penetrate. People there are supposed to be different. They're not like the harassed folk of cities, they're quite different from the kids who get ASBOs and ASBIs on the big estates of Manchester, Birmingham, Bristol or London. They're peaceful gentle people who live close to nature. They are the myth we create to stop ourselves seeing what a crazy culture we have created. Whitehaven is an urban place. It has a troubled estate, Woodhouse, built in the 1920s and 30s which underwent regeneration from 2009. The Marchon chemical works used to be close by but only the rusty gates which once let the trains from the factory through are a reminder. Over the past thirty years most of the houses have been sold off to their tenants or housing associations. Like most estates in most towns and cities, it's not a place you'd live unless you have to. You wouldn't come here looking for Old England, nor for close-knit communities. It's on the route Derrick Bird followed on the morning of 2nd June.

Woodhouse doesn't fit at all with the view of West Cumbria paraded in the media since the killings. It has never been mentioned. No-one has even hinted that this part of the world is touched by the same economic and social problems as the rest of Britain. Whitehaven used to be a mining town. As early as 1670 Sir John Lowther was developing the industry. Over a period of three hundred years seventy pits were sunk in the area. Five hundred men died in pit disasters. As recently as 1947, a hundred and four men perished in an accident at William Pit. Old England. Rolling hills. Close knit communities. David Cameron's perfunctory visit to Cumbria to express sympathy, shake policemen's hands and trot out the cliché that we may never know what made Derrick Bird flip, is typical of the behaviour of our elite. Cameron can have little idea how it feels to grow up and live somewhere like Whitehaven if you come from the working-class and are ill-educated. The papers have inevitably run articles by psychiatrists who talk of Bird's paranoia, his acting out, how the killing would have briefly relieved him of his low self-esteem. But Derrick Bird, Birdy to his mates, was an ordinary bloke. Is this our collective mind? Are we all quietly paranoid, do we act out fantasies to lift us from our poor self-esteem, do we harbour murderous desires to those closest to us, are we capable of suddenly doing terrible violence to strangers?

Perhaps the inexplicability of what happened on 2nd June lies in its likelihood. We don't believe it can happen because it will, and that is so terrible we escape into myth. If we were to admit that Hungerford, Dunblane and West Cumbria are the kind of events a culture like ours is going to throw up from time to time, we could hardly continue to believe in sleepy little communities constituting the real England. These terrible mass killings by deranged individuals, haven't happened in the expected places. You may be safer in Whalley Range than Whitehaven. One important fact about Whitehaven, of course, is that it isn't multi-ethnic. That's why it can be recruited to the myth of Old England, real England. Indigenous white folk live here. Good old Anglo-Saxons. There are no race riots in Egremont or Seascale. None of the tensions, therefore, of the big cities or the little towns of East Lancashire, once proud working-class communities where employment has collapsed and resentment of immigrants is an easy response. But Birdy was a Cumbrian born and bred. Why wasn't he content? Why was he a tortured man? And why is a tortured man an ordinary bloke?

The things that drove Birdy over the edge are experienced by millions in our society whether they live in Finchley or Frizington: family breakdown, loneliness, money worries, excessive use of alcohol, seething resentments, constant petty humiliations that accumulate till they feel overwhelming. Birdy was an ordinary bloke. He tinkered with his car in front of his house. He drank with his mates in the pub and liked the crack. He went scubadiving. Your neighbour may be the next to pick up a gun and go ape. The reason we've responded with collective bewilderment and have striven so hard to elaborate the myth of Cumbrian Old England, is that our culture is constantly pushing people to the edge but we don't want to believe it. Side by side with a worrying budget deficit and national debt is record personal indebtedness. Mr Micawber is right: to be sixpence this side of debt is psychologically vital. To be six pence the other side is to be undermined. Money is not a thing, as was pointed out long ago, it's a social relation. To owe someone money is to be in their power, unless, as Balzac pointed out, you owe them so much they are in yours. Birdy was worse than in debt: he owed money to the Inland Revenue. He was a tax evader and they were coming after him. Though he'd accumulated a tidy £60,000, his savings would be wiped out. His brother David, a manual worker like his father, lived in a £500,000 farmhouse because he'd engaged in a bit of lucky land speculation. Birdy lived in a £90,000 terrace. To be kind, you'd call it modest. To be honest you'd say it was down at the bottom end: a front door straight onto the street, no nice bay window. Dull, drab. Not many people in Whitehaven or indeed in West Cumbria live in properties worth £500,000. To have that kind of house in this part of the world is to be rich. This may seem laughable to David Cameron with his £2.5million London town-house and his £750,000 home in his constituency, but Whitehaven is not the Home Counties. There are no stockbrokers, commodity traders, million-pound-per-annum bankers. Cumbria is remote from the centres of power even if it was chosen for the digital switchover. Birdy had been hit hard. After his divorce he didn't manage to establish another relationship. He had a record for minor crime. He didn't earn much. He tried to better himself by cheating the taxman (like the rich). He made a fool of himself over a Thai prostitute. Life had dealt him a poor hand. His resentment grew. He hated his mother and told one of the women he paid for sex in Thailand he was going to get a gun and kill all those who'd wronged him. Futile to point out that objectively the wrongs weren't great. Like the Billy J. Kramer fantasist I met in Ambleside in 1965, Birdy was engaged in what John Keats called: the pursuit of identity in a world of circumstance. The only identity he could find was what we sweetly call, after our American cousins, "loser".

We are an urban people who live in atomised communities. If Old England existed, there would be no way back to it. Emma Bovary believed that certain places on earth must produce happiness, like a plant which flourishes in a particular soil. We cling to similar delusions. Geographical community and identity. The wealth enjoyed by David Cameron and George Osborne is impossible without the urban life which atomises and alienates. The rich, like Willie Whitelaw, prefer big houses in the country with lots of land and the pretence they represent real England. Urban life forces us to create new forms of community, not close-knit and based on topography, but loose, wide and founded on shared preoccupations and interests. How was Birdy to do that? How was he to find a viable identity in his very limiting circumstances? We shouldn't be surprised that people find unbearable the pressure of being exhorted to aspire while experiencing themselves as "losers". We shouldn't be surprised when they flip. Nor should we be surprised if they happen to come from little towns in Cumbria. One thing's certain: what happened on 2nd June will happen again and we shouldn't be surprised if the perpetrator comes from a village in the Cotswolds or a sleepy town in Dorset. If your neighbour shakes your hand and says there's going to a rampage, if your friend says he won't see you again, if someone you know to own guns starts to behave oddly or say weird things, be on the safe side, warn the authorities.

In October 1985 I spent my honeymoon in Outgate near Hawkshead. We had a little cottage. A piece of Old England. My colleagues poked fun saying we'd get a week of rain, but the days were clear and cold. We walked the hills, had lunch in pubs, cream teas in little cafés, dinner in *Quince and Medlar*, Cockermouth, before going back to light the coal fire in the cosy living-room. Idyllic, for a week. But after 2nd June I was very glad I didn't take the job in Whitehaven.

# The Love Killers: Thoughts on Dyadic Death
## *Rod Madocks*

*I am the love killer,*
*I am murdering the music we thought so special,*
*that blazed between us, over and over.*
*I am murdering me, where I knelt at your kiss.*
*I am pushing knives through the hands that*
*created two into one.*

**Killing The Love**, Anne Sexton

They called it 'Dyadic Death' in the trade. The forensic psychiatry trade that is. The term referred to murder followed by a suicide, usually of close family. Sometimes the victims cooperated with those that killed them, most often they did not. The descriptor 'dyadic' had an oddly poetic ring to it. It referred to the twin nature of the deed. It was a twofold crime. Death as the opposing face to love. Dyadic killers rubbed out their own marriages, families, partnerships and love affairs. It came from the Greek *dýo* meaning *'two'*. The victims and perpetrators twinned in death as they were in life.

I first came across the phenomenon during a homicide enquiry. The victim had been known to us as a patient at the mental health unit where I had worked. The couple had been married twenty years. There were no children. He worked at a light engineering firm and she kept house and suffered from chronic depression. They had a pet dog and took canal boat holidays. The medical notes concentrated on her symptoms and offered little to explain the tragedy. We never could really find out the nature and quality of their relationship. She was found dead in bed with a pillow over her face. He had shot her with a 12 bore through the pillow. You could see the hair and blood stains on the bedding and some spattering on the wall behind. The dog had also been killed; they found it in the garden shed. The husband's body was in the basement but he hadn't used the gun. He had chopped his own head off. He must have spent days constructing an extraordinary guillotine-like device. It was formed out of a lattice of wooden rails containing an inner channel slicked with car grease. He had attached the apparatus to the outside of his house from the first floor all the way down to the basement. He'd fashioned a weighted blade made of sheet metal with a breeze block attached, then he had lain with his head sticking out of the basement window looking up at the mechanism like Robespierre. He had pulled a cord that released the falling slicer. It had zipped down the lubricated channel and had taken his head straight off. It had all worked very well. He must have rehearsed the whole business. One wonders what the neighbours must have thought of the odd structure that he had so painstakingly pinned to the outside of his house. There was no explanatory note — dyadics rarely left one. For them the act was the message.

Why did this happen? We enumerated the possible reasons: the threat of impending redundancy, the inability to make his wife better from her mental ill-health problems — a sort of mercy killing? Perhaps the husband felt could no longer protect her. Maybe she wanted to leave him. Or it was a *folie à deux?* We came to no particular conclusions in the enquiry. There was not enough to go on. Those grim crime scene photos stayed with me though. Suicides always left a grievous trail. They may have swallowed up their enemy but they made sure everyone else was in a mess. That strange guillotine that the husband had made seemed emblematic of the way that suicides were obsessed by means and processes to destroy. As Anne Sexton, observed "Like carpenters they always seem to want to want to know *which tools.* They never ask *why build."* Anne herself, of course, was to kill herself eventually by means of booze, pills and car exhaust.

That guillotine husband had pronounced sentence and executed his wife and pet and then himself. The case seemed to speak to me about the essential differences between men and women and the savage consequences when things went awry between them. I felt that domestic murders never got the attention they deserved. They often seemed far crueller than serial killing. I'd never come across a female dyadic killer. There may have been some but it seemed essentially to be a male crime. Women quite often killed their children but they were hard-wired to survive themselves. Men always seemed to be riding that road from hubris to nemesis. The times had eroded the old models for masculinity yet ultimately the old cavemen came stumbling out again.

Each period had its murders; they changed like social fashions and somehow reflected the nature of each age. In the nineteenth century it was poisonings and axe murders and then came the seaside and trunk murders of the 1920s and 30s. We had seen the rise of the sex killers and serial murderers since the Second World War. Spree killings like the Columbine massacre and the Derrick Bird 2010 Cumbrian shootings seem to be the key murder mode of the present. In their indiscriminate raging they grab the headlines. Somehow, everyone can instinctively identify with those killers while also condemning them. Those shooters are acting out Gaugin's famous phrase, "Life being what it is, one dreams of revenge."

But maybe unrecognised, much less publicised, a humbler but equally determined and ferocious type of killer has really all this time been forming the true signature murder of our times.

\*\*\*

You can see a figure in the grey camera pictures, a bulky middle-aged man trundling purposefully to and fro.

There are things in his hands. The night images are murky and hard to make out. He is holding something, a bucket probably full of a mix of oil and petrol. He also holds a brick-like object. It's a power pack for the high intensity light clamped to his rifle. The gun is also in his hands. It is a .22 rimfire with a silencer and telescopic sights. A lamper's gun, designed to eliminate vermin at night. A glow begins to show from the buildings that he has just vacated. He has just done something terrible.

*Security camera pictures at Osbaston House on the night of 15th August 2008* © West Mercia Police

That was Christopher Foster. He was something of an archetype. The security camera video was released by the police in 2008. It documented Foster as he went about his work. A rare glimpse of a dyadic killer in action.

Foster was a self-made man. He started life in modest surroundings in the West Midlands selling pizza boxes and home insulation. Seemingly just an ordinary bloke until he had a brainwave in the late 1980s about how to improve fire insulation by means of a unique layering system. There had just been a disaster in the North Sea. The Piper Alpha gas rig had blown and the resulting fires had killed 167 men. Foster's insulation idea would ensure that oil and gas valve gear could be better protected in the event of a blaze in the future. Foster called his new company Ulva Systems. His products quickly became highly rated by the industry and the money rolled in. He became a millionaire and soon moved his wife Jill and his young daughter Kirstie to a newly built luxury house on the outskirts of Wolverhampton. In 2004, becoming even more confident, he paid over a million pounds cash for Osbaston House, a Georgian mansion set in sixteen acres at Maesbrook near Oswestry, close to the Welsh Borders. Jill had noticed the place only a week before they bought it, advertised in *Shropshire Life*. It was situated in a rural area for the upwardly mobile, full of mansions for Birmingham businessmen who had made it good. Here Foster could iron out his Black Country accent and reinvent himself as a country squire.

After settling into Osbaston House there followed four years of lavish spending and hobnobbing with the moneyed country set. Foster gave a quarter of a million to local antique dealers to furnish the place in a stately home style. They cheated him though, mainly setting him up with cheap copies and repros. He would pay out as much as £4,000 a day on shooting trips. He spent a fortune on hand-made shotguns and all sorts of manly toys. Of course there was a fleet of expensive cars. He cultivated a free spending image and was nicknamed *El Supremo* by his shooting buddies. He indulged his daughter's love of horses and built up a ménage and stable block as well as taking her and her horses about the country to gymkhanas and events with their large

Mercedes horse box. Despite the continued success of Ulva Systems Foster's spending outstripped his income. He seemed unable to pull back from the heroic lifestyle he had created and started to make business mistakes. He fell out with his accountant. He threatened the man who responded by informing on him to the Inland Revenue. Foster owed the Revenue hundreds of thousands in undeclared income. The pressure came on and the bills heaped. He began to borrow on the security of the house and cut corners with his suppliers, trying to buy cheaper goods in the US and pass them off as the same product. His UK suppliers took him to court and he lost the case. The judge described him publicly as, "bereft of the usual instincts of commercial loyalty". Impending ruin threatened but Foster's close family seemed not to be aware of it. The receivers froze his assets and bailiffs were due to call at Osbaston House on the day after the late summer public holiday in 2008 yet Foster continued as if nothing was going to change. He bragged about lucrative deals he was conducting and continued to roar off to shooting parties in his expensive cars.

There were some signs of trouble though. A heaving beneath the surface. He'd begun to hint to his shooting buddies that Russian gangsters were after him, vaguely alluded to threats and plots. He managed to tell his GP he was feeling suicidal but the seriousness of it was not recognised. He had no close friends in whom he could confide. He bought his mother a sensible little car at about this time and had told her that it would see her through. That uncharacteristically modest investment in her future might have indicated that something was amiss. Still, little else showed and life at Osbaston House continued much as usual.

It was August Bank holiday, 2008. On the Friday before the weekend the housekeeper said that Foster had dug out his old wedding videos and photo albums and looked at them with his wife. The couple were apparently tearful. In hindsight we wonder at those tears. How much did Jill know? Did she recognise that something was about to happen? On the Monday the family went to a friend's house for clay pigeon shooting and a barbecue. We can see them in a photo taken on that day. We can look at what was and what was soon not to be. The family sit at a linen-covered table smiling to the camera. Father and daughter have the same sloping, wary, pale eyes. His smile has a hint of grimace if you look carefully. The submissive females mirror his body posture. There is a unity about them, superficially relaxed but with a slight crouching posture as if tensing themselves from something coming from behind. Their hosts described them all as behaving normally and seemingly happy. Foster apparently even larked about. There is no end to the detachment of these men. Maybe he felt he could let go once he had decided what he was going to do. The security camera footage remains of their return at 8.45pm. Their figures are like negatives in the night images, walking shadows. You can see the figure of Foster moving away into the grounds, hands in pockets, dogs at his feet. The women go into the house carrying picnic boxes. Although the camera had made them into spectral shapes they were still living beings, still with all the choices in the world. Seven hours were left.

*Christopher Foster, wife Jill and daughter Kirstie, photo taken the day before the tragedy*
Photo courtesy of West Mercia Police

He apparently started in the early hours of that following morning. Kirstie had been exchanging messages on MSN with friends on the computer in her bedroom. She told them by phone texts that father had cut off the internet at about midnight. She said she was afraid to put it on again because, "Dad is too close." The messages ended at about 1.00am. He probably shot his wife first in the back of the head with the .22 while she was sleeping. We are not sure how he killed Kirstie. It is likely she was shot in the same way but she may have been awake. The gun was silenced but still there must have been an explosive thudding sound when he fired at Jill. There would have been the clacking of the bolt with a new round going into the chamber. Kirstie might have been alerted. He would have needed the bright muzzle light on his gun to pick her out as she ran from him in the darkened corridors of the mansion. Her remains were found corresponding to where her bedroom was situated so it is possible that he caught her in there or put her back under the covers after killing her.

Foster went downstairs, moving methodically to and fro. You can see him in the security camera striding out the front colonnaded doors to a stable block across a gravelled drive. He shot Kirstie's three horses, Scrumpy Jack, Breezy and Bramble in their stalls. They found the bullet tracks in their heads later. You can see his two Labradors and the springer spaniel milling confusedly around him as he moves in the courtyard. Next, he took them into the wired kennel compounds, killed them there and dragged their carcasses to the stables. leaving looping blood trails. That was to be the only blood found on the scene afterwards. He fired the stables after sprinkling accelerant from his bucket. One of the horses must have been still alive. They found smoke in its trachea. There are the flittering shapes of Jill's white doves, just to be made out tumbling from the blazing stables into the night. You can see him unhurriedly driving the horse box to his pillared drive entrance. He jammed the vehicle there and shot out the tyres. Once more he methodically refilled his bucket and sprayed fuel over his collection of luxury cars, dune buggies, tractors and diggers. He soaked everything down to a go-kart then set it all alight. He dragged a heavy flexible pipe, connected it to an oil heating tank and drained it through a lower floor window, filling the cellars of Osbaston House with flammable liquid. The figure retreated to the front portico of his house. Foster seemed to brandish the rifle in a last defiant gesture then disappeared inside. He bolted and barred the windows and must have splashed more petrol and oil about the house.

The ensuing conflagration ripped through the place consuming all those elaborate draperies, the faux Georgian antiques and his collection of £30,000 Purdey shotguns. Foster, it is thought, went upstairs to the third floor master bedroom and lay down on the bed next to Jill's body. Their remains were found locked together, all coiled around with the charred bedsprings. He died of smoke inhalation. A fallen chieftain immolated with his household and animals. The neighbours began to call 999 at 4.10am. The rescue services could not subdue the inferno for three days because he had blocked off their access so effectively. Everything valuable was consumed despite the efforts of twelve fire crews. Foster had left a burnt offering to his creditors. He must have ensured the security camera was running as a last testament to his determination. He was telling them, *I have built all this and now I have taken it away.* The bailiffs arrived the next day to be confronted by the scene of destruction. The bodies were not discovered for days. Kirstie's remains were only found in powdery fragments scraped up by hair brushes by the forensic team. They sifted through four tons of dust and rubble from her bedroom area but found very little of her. The great heap of plaster, ash, shredded clothes and paper contained more of her than that which they buried. The funeral and interment was held at the local church. They buried Foster separately from his two victims at the family's request. The ash heap from

Kirstie's bedroom was eventually spread in some woodlands where she used to ride.

*Torched cars at Osbaston House*
© Christopher Mitchell www.cm-photography.co.uk

Some hints came out later. Clues to the real man beneath the blustering façade. The younger brother Andrew, who had spoken out in early news reports and the coroner's court about failures in health services not spotting the risk. He later disclosed that Foster had sexually abused him in childhood. Chris had been the dominant sibling. He was called "Little Nero" by the father. He apparently constantly tormented his brother both sexually and physically. Foster had also reportedly been fascinated by fire and had even set his brother alight when they were young. The two siblings were estranged and didn't speak for fifteen years. Andrew was always afraid of Foster and knew what harm he could inflict.

Foster had also shown a tendency to act as an executioner. He had apparently shot a Labrador called Holly belonging to Kirstie. It had worried some sheep and he could not control it. He also potted his wife's pet doves when they went near his cars (one wonders what happened to the other doves which escaped from the flaming out-buildings; the only survivors of the whole holocaust). Accounts of five or six of Foster's mistresses came out out as well as stories of his rages when Jill and Kirstie learned to keep well away from him. There is evidence of him plotting to get rid of his business rivals and threatening to kill his errant accountant. There was a violence to him throughout his life although he appeared to be a doting father. You can see many images of him with Kirstie in the charred photos which still lay heaped on the kitchen sideboard after the fire. He had told friends that they had moved to Osbaston House to protect Kirstie. Apparently he would not allow her to go riding alone in their grounds. He'd always be standing there in the woods watching her. "Dad is too close," was one of her last text messages to her friends. An ambiguous figure, protector and controller.

Maybe he had a personality disorder. Maybe he was a narcissistic, highly dominant male all wrapped up in power and control issues. Perhaps he had constructed a myth for himself that he could not abandon. It's easy to find labels yet none of them seem to explain the totality of his rampage.

The ruin of Osbaston House remained untouched for four or five years as enquiries and the processes of law ground on. The police guarded the place and drove off journalists and curiosity seekers. No-one wanted any more trouble in the well-heeled environs of Maesbrook. Ulva Systems went back into business with the oil companies. Someone else was getting all the money. Four years after the crime some extraordinary photographs leaked onto the net. There is a site called UK Urban Explorer which posts images taken in forbidden buildings. Usually the daring photographers break into the places to take their images. One photographer managed to get into Osbaston House and he captured some very haunting images. His pictures show all the non-valuable things the fire had spared, the scorched fake vintage furniture with the veneer peeling back to show its softwood core, the unfashionable leather sofas, the shoddy kitchen fittings, the clothes of the victims all tumbled about, vases of artificial flowers, the rusting innards of a whirlpool bath, Kirstie's mug that says *Funky Girl* on it, Jill's lists of menu notes for meals that never would happen, jars of food still in the cupboards, tubes of toothpaste, piles of shooting magazines and most spooky of all — pictures of the kennels still standing, the shiny aluminium dog bowls still there. The ivy was boiling in through the glass-less windows of the wrecked house yet other things looked as if held in time moments after the fire. They were like artefacts in a second-rate Pompeii. There was a great sadness to the pictures that transcended the thrill-seeking purpose of their making. Those poor wrecked artefacts breathed out the melancholy reality of the crime. They called out from the victims, Jill and Kirstie. Not to be given a chance to grow old, not to rise to life's challenges. Dispossessed of life by the diktat of one who thought he knew best. Shot in the back of the head, not faced. Literally, loved to bits by Foster.

You can see in one image of the soot-stained bookshelves of what was once a study, preserved by chance, a well-thumbed copy of John Irving's *World According To Garp*. The themes of that novel involve the fear of death, and the enacting and re-enacting of the destruction of loved ones. Is also about obsessive protectiveness and how we are drawn to the things that we fear most happening. Seeing that book made me most angry with Foster. Foster was an autodidact like John Irving, yet he had learned nothing.

There are very few that survive a dyadic death scene. Sometimes a bungled suicide leaves the male crippled in the ruins or occasionally the woman survives an attack with lethal intent. Usually the killers do a good job of it though. It is estimated that one family a week is killed by a father in the US. The prevalence of dyadic death occurs at a relatively stable rate compared to the fluctuating homicide rates. The crime has the predictability of the atomic clock. It seems as if it is an indicator of something

*Debris at Osbaston House*
© Christopher Mitchell www.cm-photography.co.uk

at the heart of our relational arrangements. There are about thirty such killings a year in Britain. Murderers in Britain generally tend to be aged around 28 but male dyadic killers average out at 49 years old. 96% of them are white. Compared to male on male murderers, dyadics are also more likely not to have criminal background and to be well educated. So, they are ordinary Joes, middle-aged baby-boomers who get to the situation of killing as the only way left to accomplish being men. They would rather die than emotionally or practically confront their problems. They put the finger up to the world of health and safety, political correctness, rule of law and all the careful feminised ways of our civilisation. At the end they decide to be "real men" and not drones. There are some who even think them admirable.

What was Foster's fantasy? All the violent ones have a fantasy: a rehearsal in the mind, a milling about of thoughts which then begin to coalesce around a scenario that they play and replay in the mind. Did he play out the obliteration of his family or was it the revengeful acts of angry burning and destruction that he dwelt on? In an effort to be charitable I thought for a while that Foster had got pushed into it by drinking that Monday night, filling himself with alcohol until he could not control the destructive impulses. But no, studying the camera tapes, it's obvious he was completely in command of himself.

I know what the forensic psychiatrists would say about the Foster crime. They'd pronounce that it was a catathymic crisis. The term has been used by psychiatry since the 1930s. It is derived from the Greek *kata* for 'reversal or degeneration' and *thymos*, which refers to emotions. It describes how an emotionally charged idea temporarily overwhelms a person and pushes him off balance. Emotion trumps logic. A person acquires an idea that he believes he must carry through to a violent act. That person develops a plan and feels a tremendous urge to put that plan into action, imbuing the violence with symbolic meaning. His thinking acquires a delusional quality, marked by rigidity and poor logical coherence.

The forensic theoreticians have worked out eight stages of the catathymic crisis. It plays out in the following way, although not everyone gets through to the last one:

Following a traumatic experience, an unsolvable internal state leads to emotional tension.

— The person projects blame for this tension onto an external source.

— His thinking becomes more egocentric and self-protective.

— Violence is perceived as the only way out, so he crystallises a plan.

— To safeguard the personality, the extreme emotional tension culminates in the violent crisis, either acted out or attempted.

— The tension is relieved.

— Superficial normality occurs and that person can achieve peace.

— Inner equilibrium is recovered, with the development of insight.

There you have it, the psyche described as a mechanism. No doubt it could fit the Foster scenario. Though that moment of peace was short-lived for Foster as he laid his gun down and crawled onto his marital bed. Action had removed all contemplation, his peace was just smoke and obliteration. That's how the forensics explain it but it still seems mysterious. It is frustrating to have the crime explained as a process. It's dissatisfying and somehow too glib.

More concretely, it could just be in the hormones. Maybe catathymic processes are simply an extreme form of male thinking. Maybe dyadic males are all pumped like athletes in response to stress but it's the wrong hormone to help them sort out their problems. They really don't need all that testosterone and cortisol triggering them to fight or flight and ramping up their risk-taking.. It makes me think of the Chris Benoit case. He was a world famous Canadian wrestler, nicknamed *The Crippler*. He dominated the American professional wrestling scene with his powerful squat body and bulldog features. One day in 2007 he didn't turn up to a bout in Texas. He rang his wrestling buddies to say his family was ill. He was found later dangling from his home gym weight machine. They also found the bodies of his wife and seven year old son. He had strangled his wife with a ligature from behind, then after drugging his son with a tranquilliser, he had manually strangled him. He left a Bible next to each body. He then took three days to kill himself by hanging off his gym equipment. In autopsy, his body was found to be full of the synthetic testosterone cyprionate. It had strengthened him physically but had reduced his impulse control. Investigators could find no other reasons for the deaths.

Meaning often consists not in things but in their relationships. Looking at those photos of Osbaston House I felt like an archaeologist sifting in a ruined cave for clues to a vanished life. I found myself mentally sorting out items in that debris to see what they told me about the inhabitants. I'd become suspicious of narrative and kept going over the artefacts, moving them around in my mind. There were the remains of male things and female ones. Old popped-out shotgun cartridges, the rusted dog chains and the hulks of cars spoke of Foster's domain. The jars of preserved fruit, filleted remnants of horse tack, the filigree of wrecked plant arrangements and pleats of clothing sticking out the rubble called from the feminine side. If they could be all pulled out they'd form a map that would show how the women of Osbaston House had tried to give life to the place but Foster had gored them down. Love had been defeated by need. Maybe that's it for dyadics. They just seem to want to dominate or go extinct or maybe do both. That's all they can gouge out on their cave walls. They seem not to be able to mediate through discourse, through humour or through embracing the feminine and the forgiving.

Foster only had one idea of himself and he held onto it like a hedgehog. He had made his place in the world and he was going to hold onto it to the end. One of his acquaintances, after his death, describes watching Foster spending his days moving his cars around his garage and drive. Just shifting them a few feet or so. He seems to have had nothing else to do. Perhaps his financial pressures had made him depressed. Depression humbles those who were once dominant. It also makes them resentful. They feel better when aggression and control returns. They can then become object-seeking and acceptable to themselves once more. That's the horrible thing about Foster. He treated everything in his life as objects. All had to be destroyed. No distinction between wife, daughter and the pets. All got a bullet in the head. Gill and Kirstie were his ultimate acquisitions. In that way Foster is an archetype for our consumerist times.

\*\*\*

Apparently you can get an oxytocin pill now which can recapitulate those cuddly 'in love' feelings without all the pain of going through the whole deal. Ah, those dyadics and our addiction to romantic love. Trouble is they take the 'til death us do part' a bit too literally. The nature of love is to go on renewing itself but the dyadics just want to murder the music. Love is the only god we have got left anyway and dyadic killers are its hard core adherents. It's also something to do with the dismantling of the masculine. There are no clubs and rituals that are exclusively for men anymore. Women have even got into combat and warfare. We also live in an age with no proper rituals of passing. That's why people leave flowers at the sites of road traffic accidents or heaping them up outside places where popular icons die unexpectedly. Dyadics also make their own shrines and pyres.

Whenever I think of dyadics I remember for some reason that odd business in eighteenth and nineteenth century Lutheran Denmark when there was a plague of suicidal murderers. Apparently it became quite frequent that when men felt suicidal they would go and randomly kill a child or a passer-by. They would be then arrested, repent and die in bliss on the execution block because Luther had said that the final moments of life were the ones that really mattered in terms of redemptive forgiveness and the bigger the crime that you seek absolution for the better. There appears to have been hundreds of these murders. The authorities tried to halt the epidemic of killings of the innocent by making the resulting executions terribly torturous in order to put off the would-be murderer-suicides by execution. They took to dropping cart wheels on condemned men's legs to shatter them and other such cruelties but it never really stopped the whole business. Ironically, only the cessation of the death penalty really stopped the plague.

Dyadics are like those crazy old Danes. In a way they are seeking the bliss of those final redemptive moments when they have trashed everything that was important to them. What redemption for Foster? By leaving the cameras running, he had asserted power over death. That's why dyadics are also kin to those jihadis, the terrorist martyrs that seek *shahada*. They are also absolutists in an age of relativity.

Even the most secular of us long for miracles. I pray for the dyadics to break out of their circles of hell. It would make us all feel more alive if we could see our ends. Looking at those photos of the Foster family at that barbecue picnic I want to reach back to the past and shout, "Wake up! Wake up and live!"

Most of all I think of all those women living with their unknowable men, all penned up in their tyrannies and absolute kingdoms. Anne Sexton spoke of her husband who had, "wiped off his eyes in order not to see my insides". Watch out for love, as the good poet says, it will wrap you up like a mummy and your scream won't be heard and none of your running will end.

# Riders on the Storm
## *Melanie McGrath*

*In 1999, two bikers were murdered outside a reunion party in Battersea. It was part of a long-running feud between the Outcasts and Hells Angels. Melanie McGrath set out to get to know the men and women behind the sensational headlines. She found people leading ordinary lives, following a code of brotherhood and honour that is in some ways admirable — it's just that they kill each other now and then.*

In a side street beside the Battersea Arts Centre in south London, there is a signpost decked with the remains of flowers. Taped to the post above the blooms, there is a sticker of a death's-head in a feathered top hat with the words "Thames Outcasts: No Surrender" written below. The flowers and the men they commemorate are both long dead, but their shadows still linger on that post, waiting for the consolation of time and the weather to release them.

A year ago, a crowd of 1,700 people — assorted rockers, bikers, old-time greasers and Teds — were partying in the Arts Centre just up the road from that signpost. Joe Brown was headlining, there was dancing and drinking. The atmosphere was smooth. Even the security guards — two of whom were themselves bikers from the Outcasts motorcycle club — had begun to dip their shoulders to the beat.

Around 9pm, a security guard spotted a tall man in Hells Angels colours moving about the dance-floor The guard turned and saw a group of Outcasts hurrying down the corridor towards a side door. Turning back, he saw about a dozen Angels massing on the dance-floor, the tall man striding out ahead of them. "It was like a Western movie," he said. "People parted to let him through." Outside the Arts Centre, in Theatre Street, Keith Armstrong, or "Flipper", a member of the Outcasts, was just arriving on his bike.

There are a dozen different versions of what happened next, but the agreed facts are these. Five or six Hells Angels approached Armstrong and went at him with iron bars, coshes and at least one knife. Armstrong was also armed, but so heavily outnumbered that he didn't stand a chance. Some years previously, he had lost a leg in a biking accident and wore a prosthetic.

Malcolm St Clair — aka "Mal" or "The Terminator" — an Outcast and a giant of a man, went to help his friend, but was hit repeatedly with a blunt instrument, most likely a hammer or the side of an axe. St Clair hit back with a knife, but was cornered and stabbed. Grievously wounded, he stumbled to the post in Theatre Street, collapsed and died. Keith Armstrong suffered a heart attack as a result of his injuries and died in hospital later that night. Mal was single. Flipper left a partner, Sue, and a son, Scott. David "Diddy" Traherne, an Outcast, and Barry Hollingsworth, an ex-Outcast turned Hells Angel, were also wounded in the fight. The whole thing, said one witness, lasted "a couple of sets of traffic lights".

The press took up the story and ran with it. Before the two dead men had even been named, some papers were predicting an all-out biker war. On one hand there was moral outrage, on the other a sense that the bikers were neanderthal thugs who deserved what they got. Mostly, there was a feeling of bewilderment. As one eyewitness remarked, "It was like something happening in a world that didn't involve me. It was self-contained."

Launching Operation Middlezoy, the police appealed for witnesses, and then for photographs and videotape of the party — a Rockers' Reunion. A few Outcasts and many members of the public gave statements. "Diddy" Traherne gave a blood sample, but refused to co-operate further with the investigation. The Hells Angels kept mum. Over the next month or so, there were dozens of arrests, and a week or so after the party, police charged Hells Angels Barry Hollingsworth, Raymond Woodward and Ronald Wait with murder.

The day after the murders, I happened to wander down to Battersea Arts Centre — it was obvious something had happened because of the police-incident tape and the flowers already strewn by the post where Mal St Clair had died. Weeks later, reading the messages of condolence, so heartfelt and so ordinary — "We love you Mal and Keith" "Rest in Peace" — I began to think that, behind the biker archetypes that were filling the newspapers, lurked another story, more truthful and, maybe, more sympathetic.

It is 45 years since American teenagers queued around the block to see *The Wild One*, and the "outlaw" biker image was born — the product of a repressive Fifties culture — a not-too-threatening symbol of rebellion. Nearly half a century on, the image persists as a reassuring definition of masculinity in a culture that is no longer quite so sure what masculinity is. Plenty of image-mongering went on in those weeks after the deaths of Mal St Clair and Flipper Armstrong, but no one was interested in the outlaws' own image of themselves. And that was what I set out to discover.

Outlaw bikers are not, as a rule, fond of the press. I phoned around and talked and pestered and, eventually, persistence paid off. There's an old-fashioned stucco pub in Crayford, Kent, that serves as a meeting point for local outlaw bikers. I've been there a couple of times with Maz Harris, the Hells Angels' press spokesman and a member of the Kent chapter for 22 years. The pub's proprietor, Pete, is a member of the Crayford Old Bastards, who are on friendly terms with the Patriots, the Renegades, the Brothers Of The Wheel, the Women In The Wind, the Celtic Warriors, the Hells Angels and a number of other clubs thereabouts. It was there that I met Steve, Gypsy,

Loner, Little John, Leigh, Vince, Gasket, Mad Dog, Big Dave and the rest. A few weeks later, I was driven to the Tottenham clubhouse of the Thames Outcasts by Kev, the president, in his old Jaguar XJS (he thought I'd make a nervous pillion rider on his Harley, and he was right). A couple of weeks after that, I spent the evening with their rivals, the London Hells Angels, at their clubhouse in Hackney.

The bikers I met there were tough men. Some played up to the image, wearing leather cut-offs and faded Levis, and sporting big guts, rat-tail hairdos and cottony beards. Others were more circumspect. Their leather gear aside, they might have passed for bankers. Most were proud, and quick to take offence. A great many showed off their egos. Only a handful were overtly aggressive, and that only briefly. (And no one, incidentally, smelled.)

There are around one million registered owners of motorcycles in this country, of whom only two thousand or so are members of renegade or "outlaw" motorcycle clubs. A little under half of these belong to one of the four big clubs, or MCs: Hells Angels (which has around two hundred members in fourteen chapters); Satan's Slaves (about the same size, with chapters mostly in Scotland and the north); the Outcasts (around a hundred and fifty members, mostly in London and East Anglia); and the Outlaws (who were founded in the Midlands in 1989, with seven clubs and a hundred and fifty members, supposedly in response to Hells Angels' attempts to control the territory). Other groups are confined to particular territories or interests. The Patriots cater to ex-servicemen; God's Squad, Tribe Of Judah and the Knights Of Antioch to Christians; Women In The Wind, the Little Sisters and the English Roses to women only. One Kent-based club devotes itself to neo-Nazis, though this kind of political affiliation is rare. Bikers are, on the whole, more interested in pool than in politics.

One of the consequences of wearing an outlaw club's back-patch is that you are compelled to insist your club is tops. Generally, this is a friendly attitude; occasionally it is not. But it is universal. Even the Tribe Of Judah is obligated to cock a snook at the Knights Of Antioch.

Though few patchers (other than Angels) would ever publicly admit it, the Hells Angels, or red-and-whites, enjoy a particular cachet. (They are Hells not Hell's Angels, because the seamstress who designed their first back-patch forgot to leave space for an apostrophe.) Not only are the Angels the oldest MC — they have been established in Britain since 1969 — they are also the template on which most other clubs are based. First formed in California in 1948, the Angels took their winged death's-head insignia from the 82nd division of the 303rd US airborne, America's most successful wartime bombers, and set themselves up along quasi-military lines. The first Angels were blue-collar men who, too young to serve, had missed out on war — that great proving-ground for manhood. They were rebels with a cause and, as George Wethern, an early vice-president of the Oakland Hells Angels, said, they thought they were building "a little army".

Much of what we think we know about the outlaw scene was originally culled from Hunter S Thompson's 1966 book on the Angels, and has been hyped up and embroidered ever since. It is often said, for example, that biker novitiates must commit rape, necrophilia, communal vomiting and chicken murder before being allowed to join an outlaw club. The truth is more prosaic. Newbies, or "prospects", are required simply to live by the rules, which are usually something like this: to own a bike of 750cc or more in running order, to join in the club's runs and rallies, to refrain from wearing the club's colours on public transport or in cars, to keep off another brother's property and bedfellow(s), and to avoid injecting drugs or grassing to the coppers or the media. All members are expected to "stand their ground", as Maz Harris puts it — to honour and protect the club's colours, at whatever cost. The colours are the godhead, the symbol of the biker faith. They are sewn on to the back of the biker's jacket and imprinted on his heart.

"You've always got your patch on, whether you're wearing it or you ain't," says Kev, president of the Thames Outcasts. In his case, this means the back-patch on his jacket, the tattooed patch on his skin and the indelible mark on his soul. The fact that St Clair and Armstrong both died wearing their colours makes a difference — if not to their fate, then to their posthumous reputations and to their current status as martyrs to the cause. Since the Battersea murders, the Outcasts have worn a side-patch bearing the names of Mal and Flipper. Their clubhouse in Tottenham has become a kind of shrine to the two men. A collection box for the dead men's families sits in the hallway. The wall nearest the bar has been papered with their photographs. Two candles throw shadows on them.

If the patch is the symbol, then the bike is the embodiment of the outlaw spirit. It doesn't have to be a Harley-Davidson, but it is better that it is. A "chopped", or customised, hog is better still. A chopped hog is like a branded horse. It bears the mark of the individual who has laboured to master it.

The Harley-Davidson company capitalises on this rebel-edge reputation to sell its bikes — average price £8,000 — to professional types with outlaw fantasies. Its catalogues brim with clichés about the solitary thrill of the road. Maz Harris, a Hells Angel, is one of its testers in the UK. And it sponsors its own club, the Harley Owners Group (HOG) which has (intentionally unrealised) pretensions to outlaw status.

Although the Hells Angel and the HOG member are a different breed, they do occupy the same planet. They both enjoy the freedom of the road. Unlike the sports-bike fan, they are not overly-concerned with speed. What is important to them is the feeling of space around them and the sense of being king of the road.

Sonny Barger, founder of the Oakland, California, chapter of the Hells Angels, and a HA hero, once said: "In the HA, we know who we are, what we are and why we are." Mastery and belonging are the watchwords of the patch club. They define a certain kind of jagged, cowboy masculinity, and a sentimental, archaic attachment to a world of oath and loyalty and honour. Myth, of course, but to the biker, real and true. As one Outcast puts it, "The rest of life just don't match up to this."

Outside the charmed circle of the club, the men of the Angels, the Outcasts and the rest are mechanics, fathers, plumbers, debtors, mortgagees and husbands. They are, in other words, altogether ordinary. But with their colours on their backs, they are kings. I witnessed this in a small way when meeting Maz Harris in a central London pub one lunchtime. When he walked up to the bar wearing his Angels colours, a sea of office workers parted to make way for him, their faces a mixture of terror and fascination.

Patchers belong to the club, and therefore to each other, with a passionate intensity. For many it is their first experience of belonging. One Angel I spoke to confessed to being bullied as a kid, "But now I'm somewhere where I feel powerful for once." The club lends each of its members the weight of the collective. And, in doing so, it makes him its willing slave. So long as he continues to belong, the club contracts to regard, respect and nurture him. And that is the real, understandable pull of the thing — its desperate and enviable camaraderie.

"You can be ugly and still be loved in a patch club," says John Smith, founder of the international Christian club, God's Squad. "Men who are natural leaders, but marginalised by culture, can exercise leadership." Followers can follow without appearing diminished. "You can be psychotic and still find stability and tolerance and a place for yourself," he says. "In fact, a few of them are." Keith Amstrong's partner, Sue, also sensed this. At Armstrong's funeral, she said, "They are a motley crew, but they were his motley crew."

One night, just before Christmas, Maz Harris took me to meet some patchers in Crayford. There was one man expected, he said, whose son had recently been murdered. The man's wife was ill and he'd had a hard time. According to Harris, "It was only the biker scene that pulled him through." The man arrived and said he had something to show us. He sat down, rolled up his right sleeve and there, running along the length of his arm, was a tattoo of his dead son. A mate of his had a smaller version done in sympathy. The friendships bikers share are often painfully forged, but they last for ever. "I want to be doing this when I'm 90," says Kev. "I want to ride up on my bike to cash in my pension."

Look at it this way: the club defines a territory — both symbolic and literal — within which its own laws apply. So far as the club is concerned, what the outlaw biker does outside that territory is his own business. If that business is dirty, so what? The world inside the MC is something else, with its own culture, its own governance and its own identity. "Our first loyalty is always to the club and to each other," says one Outcast. "Always, above everything." In sacrificing his family life or career for his club, in falling foul of the law while wearing his colours, the outlaw confirms the club's importance to him. Overblown and self-dramatising maybe, but if the outlaw is willing to die for anything, it will be his club.

Spending time with patchers requires enormous tact, even for the patchers themselves. Egos are frail, hackles are spiny. I offended an Outcast by asking if his colours were blue and pink (they are blue and mauve, a crucial distinction). The outlaw biker nation is a world of deep, if unrecognised, emotion. The club's rituals — from the cupped handshake to the annual run of club members — contain the swell of feeling, they make it manageable and give it meaning. From time to time, it is inevitable that the swell of feeling breaks its boundaries. And that's when the trouble starts.

Stu Garland, editor of the custom-bike bible, *Back Street Heroes*, says, "Biker disputes can be started by someone nicking someone else's girlfriend. Once it gets out in public, there's all sorts of face-saving." Serious fights — what the tabloid press call biker wars — are infrequent but regular. In 1983, it was the Road Rats versus Satan's Slaves. In 1992, the Road Rats fought the Cycle Tramps. Now, it is the turn of the Angels and the Outcasts. Almost invariably, men die. Even patchers admit that the disputes are essentially pointless, but they shrug and say they "just happen".

Maybe this is why it is so hard to get to the bottom of them. Short of an obvious explanation, the press constructs its own theories. Which are: that the UK Hells Angels have orders from the US to wipe out the Outcasts or else lose their charter; that HAs and Outcasts are in competition for the London drug and vice trade; that the Battersea stomp is a spillover from the Scandinavian biker wars of the early Nineties, which claimed 12 lives and ended with a truce in 1994. All these are nothing more than incendiary speculation. In truth, the signpost set with flowers holds no secrets or grand conspiracies. The Angels/Outcasts dispute that cost Mal St Clair and Flipper Armstrong their lives is almost certainly just one in an atavistic, pointless turf war.

The current fracas began at the end of 1997, after the Outcasts absorbed a small trike club, the Lost Tribe. According to some, the HA convened a meeting — at which Outcasts and Lost Tribe members were both present — to discuss the matter and, presumably, to protest against what they perceived to be flagrant empire building on the Outcasts' part. According to others, the Lost Tribe was part of a wider Outcast scheme to increase its membership. In any case, the Outcasts say that at the meeting the Angels barred them from riding across HA territory in groups of more than four. The Angels deny this.

Shortly afterwards, twenty-two Outcasts defected to the Hells Angels. The Outcasts say that one of the defectors was power-crazed and had ambitions beyond his station. They had taken on a number of recruits who had proved fickle and willing to be led by him. It didn't help that the HA offered the defectors promises of loans for bikes. The HA say the defectors simply recognised a superior MC and deny that there were loans. "We don't go looking for members," says Maz Harris. "They come looking for us."

One HA sympathiser told me, "The Outcasts still think they are living in the Seventies." (A time when the outlaw scene was more openly sectarian.) Whatever the truth, each side accused the other of intimidation. And on January 31, 1998, Keith Armstrong and Mal St Clair lost their lives.

Violent death is a commonplace of outlaw life. So many die in traffic accidents that their clubhouses have walls decked with the dead men's pictures. Shaun Stillman, UK president of the Christian patch club, God's Squad, officiated at four patcher funerals last year, including the remembrance service for Mal St Clair. It was held in a Methodist chapel in Tooting, south London, after a number of churches nearer St Clair's home in Catford refused to have anything to do with him. Stillman was one of 200 bikers who showed up at Keith Armstrong's funeral in Manor Park Crematorium, east London. "Keith was just in the wrong place at the wrong time," said his father, Bob.

One year later, the feud rumbles on. Last summer, a fertiliser-based bomb was found at the Hells Angels clubhouse in Luton, and Maz Harris's bike shop in Kent was firebombed. In June, two Outcasts were shot leaving a pub close to their clubhouse in Bow, but refused to co-operate with the police. The Angels say, "We've had to look at ourselves and the image we present." The Outcasts say that their lives have dimmed: "We don't have the social events we used to, and it has increased the pressures at home from our old ladies."

In July, the National Criminal Intelligence Service (NCIS) warned of possible "armed conflict and the use of automatic weapons and explosives" by Outcasts at the HA's annual Bulldog Bash rally at Long Marston.

According to Maz Harris, who organised the Bash, NCIS informed the HA that it had the names of 15 suspects and traced an amount of Semtex, but then refused to substantiate the claim. "We never discuss intelligence reports," says an NCIS spokesman. Warwickshire Police asked the Angels to cancel the event, but they refused. The Bulldog Bash went ahead under heavy police guard, at a cost to the public of around £140,000. There were no explosions and no arrests. In fact, in the 12 years the Bulldog Bash has been running, there has never been an arrest on site.

A month later, NCIS informed Essex Police and the Motorcycle Action Group (MAG) — a respectable lobbying organisation which sponsors the Braintree-based Magna Carta rally — that "120 armed criminals" were planning to drop by. Again, the information was unsubstantiated and, again, the police asked the organisers to cancel the meet, which they did, at a loss to MAG of £40,000.

NCIS has had the outlaw scene in its sights since its inception in 1992. In 1994, NCIS called the Hells Angels "the fastest-growing organised-crime group in the world", and accused them of "involvement in drug-trafficking, contract killing, extortion, prostitution, money laundering and credit-card fraud". Sources estimate that up to one-third of NCIS's annual budget — last year, it was £35,928,000 — is spent on gathering intelligence about outlaw bikers. NCIS won't discuss the figure.

In all that time, and with all that money, NCIS has never been able to prove that Hells Angels operate as an organised crime gang in the UK. Undoubtedly, some patchers are involved in crime; they themselves admit it. Even Maz Harris will agree that it was Hells Angels who murdered St Clair and Armstrong. But none of this amounts to evidence that the Hells Angels, or any other patch group, are engaged in organised crime or represent a threat to society. John Smith, president of God's Squad, has lived and worked on the outlaw bike scene for 30 years. He is an award-winning human-rights campaigner. He notes that, "In clubs with international chapters, there will be some passing on [of criminal activities], but these guys are not the Mafia."

NCIS has pulled back since its inflammatory statement of 1994. "At no stage has anybody said that all Hells Angels are engaged in crime. All we're saying is among Hells Angels are people who commit crime on a sophisticated and regular basis," insists a spokesman. No patch club would be likely to argue with this. They would simply point out that the same could be said of bankers, mechanics or journalists. At his funeral, Keith Armstrong's partner Sue said, "When I met Keith, he told me that if women were a mystery then men were a crime story."

None of this is of any help to Mal St Clair, Keith Armstrong or their families. To date, no one has been convicted of their murder. The case against Hollingsworth and Woodward was withdrawn after police accidentally revealed the names of two protected witnesses to the solicitor for the defence, and the two witnesses in question, an Outcast and his wife, refused to give evidence. Essex Hells Angel Ron Wait was convicted of conspiracy to cause grievous bodily harm and sentenced to 15 years. The murder charge against him was dropped after the jury failed to agree a verdict.

I often think of the Outcasts, shooting pool in their dingy, low-slung clubhouse hung with camouflage nets, the pictures of Mal and Keith on the walls and the candles burning beneath. And I think of the Hells Angels in their clubhouse in Hackney, drinking Bud beside the plaques commemorating their past runs and anniversaries, beside the stuffed cougar head, the hangman's noose, the pinball machines and the pictures of their dead. Back in the Sixties, Hunter S. Thompson wrote that, "beyond the initial strangeness [the outlaw bikers'] everyday scene is tedious and depressing". But it's no more so than most everyday scenes. It's just that there is a myth surrounding these men, and there is a part of many of us which wants that myth to be true.

Hunter Thompson said, "The main reasons the Angels are such good copy is that they are acting out the daydreams of millions of losers who don't wear any defiant insignia and who don't know how to be outlaws." Since the murders, for example, Maz Harris has become a kind of celebrity by association. People see him wearing his Angels colours in the street and ask to shake his hand. They like the danger in it. And not so long ago, a group of advertising executives contacted the Outcasts and asked to photograph them. "They came round, took a look, then said they couldn't use us because we didn't look enough like real bikers."

The outlaw biker is not a god, but he is not a devil, either. The image he presents is not only his own myth; it is ours, too. The only difference is that he is trapped in it. "It's hard to think of another life," says one Outcast. "What would you do? Go home and take up crochet?"

# Knuckling Under:
# The Politics of Police Work
# in Weimar Berlin
*Damien Seaman*

To get an idea of what it was like to be a police officer in Weimar Germany, picture this: you come to work one morning to find your boss under arrest. How do you react? Yes, I know. It depends how you feel about your boss. But this was the dilemma facing the Berlin police on 20th July 1932.

This was the day federal troops marched into police headquarters on Alexanderplatz. They were there to remove Police President Albert Grzesinski and his two deputies by force. And they did so at the behest of a national government ruling by emergency decree rather than by dint of a majority in the Reichstag.

With the gift of hindsight, we can see this event — the Papen Putsch — as a major step towards the Nazi rise to power six months or so later. As Nazi propaganda chief Joseph Goebbels wrote delightedly in his diary that day, "You only have to bare your teeth at the reds and they knuckle under." But the Nazis had nothing to do with this particular coup. Not directly. And when you strip away our knowledge of what was to come, there was little to suggest the putsch was anything more than business as usual.

Even when the Nazis first entered government in January 1933 it would have been impossible to guess that it marked a point of no return for Germany. Let me explain and you'll see why.

# The curse of political violence

The Weimar Republic was born of political violence in 1918 and remained in its shadow right up until 1933. At the end of the First World War in November 1918, revolution spread across Germany. Street fighting took hold in Berlin and other major cities. The newly-formed Communist Party tried to latch onto this spontaneous uprising and establish a free socialist republic.

Some of the police even joined the revolution, including the then police president. The social democrat government sent in the army to restore control, as well as a force of paramilitary volunteers called the *Freikorps*. When soldiers laid siege to police headquarters with heavy machine guns, unwittingly they provided the perfect metaphor for the breakdown of law and order. Government troops murdered the communist leaders Rosa Luxemburg and Karl Liebknecht in January 1919. But in a sign of what was to come, there was no question of the killers facing justice. A pattern soon emerged. While Berlin's detectives got better at solving crimes than ever before, politically motivated murders often went unpunished.

After the revolution came the short-lived Kapp Putsch of 1920 — some of the *Freikorps* attempted a military coup. The labour unions defeated them by calling a general strike. But the violence didn't end there. The early '20s added political assassinations to the mix. These peaked with an audacious murder that shook financial markets' faith in the government and helped cause the now-infamous hyperinflation that crippled the German economy for a year and a half. What could cause such a reaction?

On the morning of 24th June 1922, foreign minister Walther Rathenau was on his way to work in an open-topped car. A Mercedes containing three men pulled alongside. One of the men shot Rathenau with a submachine gun. Another threw a grenade into the minister's car. Rathenau died in his chauffeur's arms.

Police arrested twelve men within weeks, though the killers died trying to escape. The conspirators belonged to a group called the Organisation Consul. Members of the group came from the same pool of *Freikorps* volunteers who'd put down the revolution in 1919 and then taken part in the Kapp Putsch of 1920.

Rathenau had offended many on the right by his willingness to negotiate over war reparations rather than oppose them outright. His Jewishness no doubt offended them too. But interestingly, during their trial, although the defendants gave several reasons why they'd targeted Rathenau, they all denied his being Jewish was one of them. This time, there was some justice. Several of the conspirators went to jail. The driver of the Mercedes got fifteen years. He only escaped the death penalty because he made the court believe he'd been forced into it against his will.

A small memorial marks the site of Rathenau's murder. It's on the Königsalle in the Grunewald suburb of Berlin. Visiting it is quite a moving experience. It's also worth a look at Rathenau's villa at number 65 Königsalle.

Despite public shock over Rathenau's death, the political violence still didn't stop. Street clashes between the Communist Red Front Fighters' League and police took place regularly. From the mid-20s on it got worse when Nazi stormtroopers (the SA) entered the fray. Even the normally law-abiding social democrats had their own paramilitary group called the *Reichsbanner*.

## The trouble with communists...

The communists often accused the police of treating them unfairly compared with other paramilitary groups. There were obvious reasons for why this should be. Firstly, they'd been an active threat for longer than the others. Secondly, the majority of police recruits in Berlin came from rural areas outside the city and proved immune to the pleas of the urban worker. Thirdly, the politicians who ran the police in Berlin were social democrats. And thanks to the bitter legacy of the revolution, the socialists hated the communists more than they hated the Nazis. To prove the point, the socialist state government in Prussia banned the Red Front Fighters' League in May 1929, a full three years before the federal government did. Lastly, the Communist Party's links with organised crime were strong, and there were many in the police who resented this.

The communists tended to base themselves in poor, working class areas. In Berlin the Communist Party headquarters was on Bülowplatz, right in the heart of the feared Scheunenviertal. This was an area filled with recent migrants from Eastern Europe. Most of them were Jewish. Few of them could speak German. Exploitation, drugs and prostitution were rife. The police didn't dare patrol the area alone.

Bülowplatz became a magnet for disturbances of the peace. Not only did the communists march in the area, so did the SA, looking to pick a fight with the reds. And as for the link between communists and organised crime, some gang members joined the Party while many of those that didn't became hired killers for them instead. No wonder Berlin detectives had a saying that though not every communist was a criminal, every criminal was a potential communist.

## Politics and murder don't mix

Ernst Gennat was an ambitious detective who joined the force in 1904 and passed his exam for the criminal investigations department in 1905. Before the mid-20s, the Berlin police had no permanent homicide squad. Instead, detectives joined special murder commissions formed on a case-by-case basis. When the cases ended, the men were moved again to other departments.

Gennat argued that a regular pool of homicide detectives would build up a body of knowledge that would help them solve murders more efficiently. He seemed to judge success by the extent to which he annoyed his superiors. In 1926 his bosses caved in. They formed the dedicated homicide department he had asked for. Perhaps hoping to see Gennat fall on his face, they also put him in charge of it. By 1931, the new department solved 108 of 114 crimes — a clean-up rate of 95%. That's higher than many modern homicide departments. Yet despite this success, the explosion of political killings in the early '30s pushed the number of unsolved murders higher.

On the morning of 19th January 1932, for example, Nazis and communists clashed at the Felseneck allotments. Two people died. Detectives spoke to over 200 witnesses but they couldn't find the killers. It was well-nigh impossible to do so when these deaths occurred during street battles, and killers and victims had no personal connections.

The coming of the Great Depression after 1929 only made such clashes worse. By 1932, unemployment in Berlin had rocketed from 133,000 to 600,000. Many of those now out of work joined the Nazis or the communists out of protest. The more frequent the clashes, the more frequent the deaths. And the harder it was for detectives to solve them. This meant older professionals such as Gennat deliberately ignored the intrusion of politics into their work. To men like this, the Papen Putsch and the arrest of the police president in July 1932 were irrelevant at best. At worst they were a damaging distraction. As was the Nazis' rise to power. Gennat never joined the Nazi Party even when it became the norm. Such was his popularity that the Nazis never pressured him to so.

The desire to remain aloof from politics and get on with the job made it easier for the Weimar Republic to crumble and for German democracy to die. Not to mention for the Nazis ultimately to change the very nature of what constituted a crime. Even there, it was hard to see a fundamental change. At least at first. That's because the toxic mix of murder and politics meant that common or garden murders got tangled up with political motives. Consider the following example.

## The death of Hitler's Jewish clairvoyant

When a farmer found a bullet-ridden body in a field north of Berlin, relatives soon identified the dead man as Erik Jan Hanussen, who'd been missing for ten days. Hanussen was a famous psychic with friends in high places. These included Count von Helldorf, the head of the SA in Berlin. Hanussen had even met Hitler and predicted a glowing political future during a much-publicised séance.

The clairvoyant fell afoul of the Nazi leadership by posing as a Danish aristocrat when he was, in fact, a Jew named Steinschneider. This was embarrassing to those such as Helldorf who had attended parties on Hanussen's yacht, the Ursel IV. Helldorf had even inducted Hanussen as a member of the SA. But the Jewish issue wasn't Hanussen's only problem.

During a séance at his Palace of the Occult on Lietzenburgstrasse he'd also predicted the Reichstag fire just one day before it happened. We now know that a Dutch communist called Marinus van der Lubbe did the deed, and that he did it alone. Yet many at the time and since believed that the Nazis started the Reichstag fire themselves. With his SA contacts, Hanussen's prediction could have been taken as inside information from just such a plot. And the Nazis couldn't have that when they were denouncing the fire as a communist conspiracy and using it as the excuse to arrest thousands of Communist Party members. Or when they had an election to fight just a week later. Such was the public outcry at the fire that any hint of Nazi involvement would have lost them votes.

Yet for all the politics, the real motive could simply have been that Hanussen had also lent large sums of money to von Helldorf, who was constantly in debt and couldn't afford to pay him back. So was this a political killing or not? The lines were so blurred it was impossible to say for sure.

The police never solved this murder. We now know that the trigger men were three members of the SA. But by the time detectives started to investigate, the Nazis were in charge of Prussia's police force. So they dropped the case amid vague public allegations of underworld links that Hanussen didn't really have. If that seems shocking, remember that Rathenau's two killers never stood trial. Remember that the soldiers who murdered Rosa Luxemburg and Karl Liebknecht never stood trial either. And while we could argue that the case of the two communists was different because they'd been trying to bring down the government, they died while in custody. Was the decision not to investigate their deaths any less a perversion of justice than the Nazis' approach to the wayward Hanussen?

And if it's difficult to see a clear difference now, just how much worse was it for those fighting crime in those topsy-turvy times? Sadly, the Nazis had precedent on their side. However bloodthirsty they proved to be, the social democrats and communists had shown them the way. Or, to put it another way, from the point of view of the long-suffering Berlin copper, had anything really changed?

## A house divided against itself...

So let's go back to the question at the top of this article. When Chancellor Franz von Papen ordered the arrest of Grzesinski and his deputies Weiss and Heimannsberg in July 1932, how did their men respond?

It depended, of course, on their personal bias. As we've seen, many officers distanced themselves, wanting to get on with the job. Others used this stance to disguise their dislike for the republic. These men were happy to see the republic fall. But it is hard to know how many officers felt this way. It's far easier to find out how many of them had stronger political leanings. And of those that did, they were split between supporting either the social democrats or the Nazis.

This must have made for an unbearably tense working relationship. For while the socialists and Nazis shared a common hatred of communists, they also hated each other. In some of the police precincts in Berlin, socialist supporters dominated. In others, Nazis supporters did, while still others were split down the middle. It's a wonder they managed to get any police work done at all.

The strong socialist bias is not surprising. The social democrats had run the police as an arm of the Prussian state they dominated politically. And in the 1920s the party had made it easier for working class Berliners and university graduates to join the police, increasing the number of recruits likely to vote socialist. What is curious is why the more ardent socialist policemen did not take to the streets to protest against the arrest of their bosses.

Police Colonel Magnus Heimannsberg was a popular man who'd risen through the ranks. He was also such an outspoken champion of the republic that the Nazis complained of discrimination against SA men during riots and marches. (We've already seen how Goebbels called the police "reds" in his diary.) Certainly there were those of his enemies who feared that removing him would inspire revolt. Many of the police colonel's men talked about linking up with the socialist *Reichsbanner* paramilitaries to protest. Yet they never did.

## Why no protest?

Here the attitude of the republicans might tell us why. For, while Heimannsberg and his fellow deputy Bernhard Weiss both fought their removal, they did so legally through the courts. Meanwhile Police President Grzesinski accepted his sacking. The post of police president was a political one after all, and Grzesinski a career politician in the Social Democrat Party who'd also served as Prussian interior minister.

While most of the police were either anti-Weimar or just took the Papen Putsch in their stride, the avid socialists refused to stoop to the level of their opponents and subvert the law to get their way. The republicans' faith in the legal institutions of the republic was their greatest weakness in the face of such ruthless opposition.

So we could argue that the attitude of the police helped ease the path to fascist dictatorship in Germany. But let's not forget, from 1918 to 1933 the police had seen — and seen off — many challenges. Violent but failed revolution. A background of constant political violence from right and left. Hyperinflation. Mass unemployment. Shaking your head and trying to get on with the job must have seemed the only sane choice. Especially given the instability of the federal government over the period, when each cabinet lasted an average of just eighteen months. Who was to say when von Papen's meddling would be reversed?

Even when Hitler came to power, it was as part of a coalition in which the Nazis were the junior partners. It would have been hard for them to stay in power for long. Not without the Reichstag fire and the crackdown on political opposition that followed. Or without President Hindenburg's death in 1934. And who in their right mind would have foreseen that a Dutchman would set light to the Reichstag? (Aside from Hanussen of course — and we know what happened to him.)

The party leaders themselves worried that their electoral support had peaked in 1932. There were also signs that the economy was starting to revive, which would have undermined that support all the more rapidly. There was very little, in other words, to suggest to the old hands at Alexanderplatz that the state and the very nature of crime were about to change beyond recognition. They didn't know what we know now.

Given the circumstances, would you or I have reacted any differently?

# Further reading

Clark, Christopher, *Iron Kingdom: The Rise and Downfall of Prussia, 1600-1947* (Allen Lane, London, 2006)

Evans, Richard J., *The Coming of the Third Reich* (Allen Lane, London, 2003)

Gordon, Mel, *Erik Jan Hanussen: Hitler's Jewish Clairvoyant* (Feral House, Los Angeles, 2001)

Lang, Hsi-huey, *The Berlin Police Force in the Weimar Republic* (University of California Press, Berkeley, 1970)

Papen, Franz von, *Memoirs* (Andre Deutsch, London, 1952)

Waite, Robert G.L., *Vanguard of Nazism: The Free Corps Movement in Postwar Germany 1918-1923* (Norton Library, 1969)

# The First Murderer
## John Lucas

My title comes from "Imperial Adam", a poem by the Australian poet A.D. Hope. (1907–2000). The poem ends with Eve in the last stages of her pregnancy:

> Lax on the grass; and Adam watching too
> Saw how her dumb breasts at their ripening wept,
> The great pod of her belly swelled and grew,
>
> And saw its water break, and saw, in fear,
> Its quaking muscles in the act of birth,
> Between her legs a pigmy face appear,
> And the first murderer lay upon the earth.

This is Hope's take on the originary myth of Judeo-Christianity, on which Milton drew for the opening of *Paradise Lost*. "Of Man's first disobedience and the fruit/Of that forbidden tree, whose mortal taste/Brought death into the world and all our woe/With loss of Eden." Man's fall inaugurates not merely mortality but murder.

But long before the Old Testament established Cain as the world's first murderer, Greek myths had brought death into the world of Western culture. The Greek originary myths include, in alphabetical order, fratricide, infanticide, matricide, parricide and regicide, though not, I think, suicide. Also rape, bestiality, torture, a God who knowingly devours his children and a king, Tereus, who, after raping his sister-in-law and cutting out her tongue to prevent her from speaking, sits down to a meal prepared by his wife, Procne, though unfortunately for him she has discovered her sister's fate. To avenge her, Procne kills her own son and serves him up to his father in a pie.

What is all this? Madness? Evil? No, the terms don't apply. As the great classical scholar, Moses Hadas, argues, trying to accommodate the protagonists of these myths — whether Gods or mortals — to modern notions of individuality, of conscience, of psychological complexity, makes no sense. The Oedipus complex may owe its name to a tragic tale set in pre-historic Thebes, but the Oedipus who killed his father, Laius, and married Jocasta, his mother, was merely fulfilling the prophecy of the Oracle. There's no avoiding fate. Even the formidable scholar G.S. Kirk, who wants in some measure to qualify Hadas's dismissal of the Greek heroes as fully individuated, says, in his introduction to Robert Fitzgerald's translation of *The Iliad*, that while it is wrong to claim, as some have, that "the epic tradition did not have the resources, either conceptual or linguistic, for describing mental tensions or even the process of making up one's own mind", nevertheless, "psychological insight is not an ordinary or a developed tool of the epic tradition." (World's Classics p. xv). Kirk is at this point wanting to argue that Homer's Agamemnon is a complex character, although he admits that some of this complexity may in fact be due to the addition of post-Homeric material and/or the shifting about of incidents in the re-telling of the story. But anyway, Agamemnon's deeds are a given. He couldn't have done otherwise.

And this is the point. In a sense Marx hardly intended, the heroes and heroines of Greek myth are what they do. They have no choice in the matter. They suffer their fates, but whether these can be considered just punishments depends on whether, for example, we think it fair enough that a king — Agamemnon — who is told by the Goddess Artemis that the winds will not carry his ships from Aulis to Troy unless he sacrifices his daughter, Iphigenia, should do the Goddess's bidding, for which he is slaughtered by his own wife, Clytemnestra, with help from her lover, Aegisthus, when, after ten years he finally returns to Mycenae. For this, she is herself killed by their son, Orestes, egged on by his sister, Electra. Not much point in sending the social workers round to sort out *this* dysfunctional family.

It's true that according to one version of the myth Iphigenia is at the last moment saved by Artemis, who sends the girl off to be a priestess at one of her shrines. But obviously news of this never reaches Clytemnestra. In the version on which the great Greek tragedians relied, Agamemnon summons his daughter to Aulis on the pretext that Achilles wants to marry her. According to Euripides' play, *Iphiginia at Aulis*, Achilles, though resentful at having been used as a lure, decides to defend the innocent girl. But Iphiginia, anxious not to thwart her father's hopes for a successful war against the Trojans (who had made off with Helen, his brother, Menelaus's, wife), "rises to her height as the saviour of Hellas, and willingly goes to the sacrifice."

Putting it that way — as Paul Harvey does in his *Oxford Companion to Classical Literature* — allows us to infer that while classical historians and anthropologists have inevitably been endlessly fascinated by how best to interpret Greek myths, they have typically seen them as ways of accounting for and explaining the emergence and attainment of what might be called national consciousness. In such myths it may make sense to talk about crimes against the state, but in that case Agamemnon is doing his duty when he accedes to Artemis's order to kill his own daughter. Her death ensures that the Greeks can get to and finally destroy the topless towers of Troy. He does what he has to do.

Such a defence might not stand up in a modern court of law, where the plea to be only following orders — the excuse of those on trial at Nuremberg — could hardly be expected to attract any sympathy. But this is because the individual conscience is now judged to be part of what motivates actions. Such motivation can only, I think I'm right in saying, be exonerated in those who are found to be not of sound mind.

There is an obvious problem with this. Who is to decide on the soundness of mind of the accused? Here, we come up against the characteristic post-modern idea of what is sometimes called "ontological insecurity." Or, to put it in layman's terms, the problem of divided consciousness. "Psychology has split and shattered the idea of a 'Person,' and has shown that there is something incalculable in each of us, which may at any moment rise to the surface and destroy our natural balance." The words are E.M. Forster's, and they occur in his essay "What I Believe". Contrary to the assumption of those many post-modern sutlers who assert that the idea of "ontological insecurity" goes no further back than French post-war theorists, Forster was, in 1938, uttering what was already a commonplace, one that makes itself heard in Fernando Pessoa's "To be oneself is not to be," a dictum of the 1920s which the great Portuguese poet put into operation by writing under at least four pseudonyms. And behind *that* is, of course, Rimbaud's "*Je est un autre.*" From this to the post-modern claim that multiple personality disorder means that there is no "I" who can stand accused of a crime is not a mighty step.

There is, though, a huge step change implicit in the term. I can recall in the late 1990s being assured by a writer who was all in favour of such disorder as a means to creativity (or was it that creativity encouraged such disorder?) that, properly considered, no murderer can ever be guilty as charged, because there is no-one at home to *be* charged. That this is nonsense can be inferred from the fact that even the most ardent of subscribers to the belief that we are disunited identities, *in practice* behaves as though *Je suis un seul et meme.* I'm pretty sure that if I called a warning to even the most rigorous critical theorist, hoping to alert him/her that a tree was about to fall on her/him, he/she wouldn't ask which of her/his different selves I was addressing. They'd take avoiding action.

People are by and large held to be accountable for their actions. Granted, some actions are involuntary, but most are willed, including actions that go against the law. These actions are called crimes. According to the *Oxford English Dictionary* a crime is (2) "An act or omission constituting an offence (usu. a grave one) against an individual or the State and punishable by law." (The 1st definition I will set out at a later moment of this essay.) Those who commit crimes are, if caught, punished for them. This is deep within the Judeo/Christian tradition. Which is why men try to hide their criminal deeds. Agamemnon doesn't try to hide what he's done. Why should he? He's been ordered by Artemis to kill his daughter? He's not going against the Law. On the contrary, he's obeying it. A god, a god, his sacrifice rules. And you don't argue with a god.

## II

We move from Homer to the author of *Genesis*. In chapter 22 of the first book of the Old Testament, God/Jahweh tells Abraham to "Take now thy son, thine only son, whom thou lovest, even Isaac, and get thee into the land of Moriah and offer him there for a burnt offering upon one of the mountains which I will tell thee of. ... And they came to the place which God had told him of; and Abraham built the altar there, and laid the wood in order, and bound Isaac his son, and laid him on the altar, upon the wood. And Abraham stretched forth his hand, and took the knife to slay his son." At which point God calls out to Abraham telling him to desist, "for now I know that thou fearest God, seeing thou hast not withheld thy son, thine only son, from me." (King James' Bible verses 2–13).

When for a brief moment in World War Two Evelyn Waugh and Randolph Churchill found themselves bunking together somewhere in Europe, Waugh, who quickly became tired of Churchill's bibulous chatter, suggested to that brandy soak that he might like to take himself to bed and read the Bible. Churchill, who it seems had never previously opened the Good Book, did as Waugh suggested, but it brought Waugh little peace. All night long the air was rent with loud cries of "God, what a shit God is." Although Waugh does not specify which passages of the Bible brought on Churchill's scatological fury, it's difficult not to believe that *Genesis*, 22 would have been one of them.

And yet Abraham himself utters no protest at what he's commanded to do. Is he then no different from Agamemnon? But to ask this is to ask the wrong question. The right question has to be: is Abraham's God no different from Artemis? The answer to this question is, of course, yes, there is a huge difference, or anyway, a huge difference is intended by those who set down the Old Testament. The God of Judeo/Christianity is a good God. It is the Gods of the Ancients who are the real shits. They are cruel, capricious, their topmost God thinks nothing of coming down to earth disguised as a bull, a swan, a shower of gold, in order to rape innocent girls who are then shown no mercy by the topmost God's jealous wife; these gods make impossible demands of the humans who worship and build temples to them, they war among themselves, they sulk, cheat on each other, they are by turns feckless and brutal, and there is no certain way of pleasing them. Even Artemis, the shining — well, moon-like — example of chastity and, you'd have thought, restraint, arranges to have a hunter who accidentally spied on her when she was naked turned into a stag and torn to pieces by his own hounds. Given this, it should come as no surprise that she insists Agamemnon must sacrifice his daughter if he wants fair winds to blow his fleet to Troy. Why be a God if you can't order someone's destruction?

By contrast, the Judaic God *doesn't* order Isaac's destruction, not really. He is merely putting Abraham to the test. Still, Abraham doesn't know this. For all he can tell, God intends him to kill his son. (And anyone reading the story in the Christian era will inevitably see in the tale a foreshadowing of Christ's crucifixion.) So off Abraham goes to the land of Moriah, following orders. And is then excused from killing Isaac. As to what he thinks of all this, we have no idea. Nor does he say anything to God. There is no plea bargaining, no questioning of why he should sacrifice Isaac. Agamemnon is promised fair winds for putting Iphigenia to death. Abraham is promised nothing. "What's my motivation?" Paul Newman is supposed to have asked Alfred Hitchcock of a scene he was to play in *Torn Curtain*. The reply was short and to the point. "Your wage packet." Abraham's motivation is simply doing God's will. There is no wage packet. There is no hint of a reward of the kind Artemis promises Agamemnon. Yet Abraham doesn't protest, doesn't even query God's order. A faithful servant, he is what he does.

## III

But then what of the man Hope calls "the first murderer." Cain kills his younger brother, Abel, not because he is ordered to do so but because he is jealous of him. The motivation is in other words personal. A crime has been committed. It's all set out in *Genesis*, 4.

> And in process of time it came to pass, that Cain brought of the fruit of the ground an offering unto the LORD. And Abel, he also brought of the firstlings of his flock and of the fat thereof. And the LORD had respect unto Abel and to his offering: but unto Cain and his offering he had not respect. And Cain was very wroth, and his countenance fell. And the LORD said unto Cain, Why are thou wroth? And why is thy countenance fallen? If thou doest well, shalt thou not be accepted? And if thou doest not well, sin coucheth at the door: and unto thee shall be his desire, and thou shalt rule over him. And Cain told Abel his brother. And it came to pass, when they were in the field, that Cain rose up against Abel his brother, and slew him. And the LORD said unto Cain, Where is Abel thy brother? And he said, I know not: am I my brother's keeper? And he said, What hast thou done? The voice of thy brother's blood crieth unto me from the ground. And now cursed art thou from the ground, which hath opened her mouth to receive thy brother's blood from thy hand;

when thou tillest the ground, it shall not henceforth yield unto thee her strength; a fugitive and a wanderer shalt thou be in the earth. And Cain said unto the LORD, My punishment is greater than I can bear. Behold, thou hast driven me out this day from the face of the ground; and from thy face shall I be hid; and I shall be a fugitive and a wanderer in the earth; and it shall come to pass, that whosoever findeth me shall slay me. And the LORD said unto him, Therefore whosoever slayeth Cain, vengeance shall be taken on him sevenfold. And the LORD appointed a sign for Cain, lest any finding him should smite him. (verses 3–15.)

The key moment here is surely God's warning to Cain that he is responsible for his own actions. If he doesn't behave well, "sin coucheth at the door." He can't blame God for not showing him respect, whatever that means.\*

Byron's verse drama, *Cain*, which he subtitles "A Mystery", in conformity, a Prefatory Note tells us, "with the ancient title annexed to dramas upon similar subjects, which were styled 'Mysteries or Moralities,'" takes the murderer to be a kind of Romantic hero, as the author explained in a letter to his publisher, John Murray. "Cain is a proud man: if Lucifer had promised him kingdoms, etc., it would *elate* him: the object of the Demon is to *depress* him still further in his own estimation than he was before, by showing him infinite things and his own abasement." And from this comes the catastrophe of his killing Abel, which is done not out of envy, Byron insists, nor premeditation, but "from the rage and fury against the inadequacy of his state to his conceptions, and which discharges itself rather against Life and the Author of Life, than the mere living." (Byron, *Letters*, ed. Howarth, Dent, 1948, p. 315.)

---

\*A Jewish friend told me that while among Rabbinical scholars there is no certainty as to the sign God fixes on Cain, the commentary in her Soncino edition of the *Chumash*, 4th impression, 1962, says the mark was one of the letters of God's name. She also told me that some Southern Baptist churches asserted that the mark of Cain was being black, thus justifying slavery.

As a case for the defence, this leaves a good deal to be desired. Leslie A. Marchand, in his celebrated *Byron A Portrait*, tries to put a gloss on the matter when he says that Byron's purpose in writing the play was "to indulge in the farthest realms of speculation on questions of predestination, fate, free will, and the problem of evil." (Marchand, 1976, p 346.) Well, yes, and I can understand that Byron, raised by a mother whose Calvinistic conviction of predestination undoubtedly affected her son, was absorbed in speculations about the nature of evil and the eschatological consequences of evil acts. (None, you're damned from birth.) But were Cain to hire a modern lawyer, I suspect he'd spend some time deciding which *kind* of murder the defendant might plead guilty to having committed. Because as David Bellos notes in his entertaining *Is That a Fish in Your Ear: The Amazing Adventure of Translation*, what looks to the layman like murder plain and simple, "may be *first degree, second degree, manslaughter, homicide*, or even *collateral damage*." (Penguin Books, 2011, p 225. The italics are Bellos's.)

The term murder, in other words, covers a multitude of sins. Not for Cain's God, it has to be said, and indeed in the King James version, Cain isn't even called a murderer. He is a slayer. Nevertheless, he is guilty of the crime of fratricide, and in the eyes of God he is therefore a sinner. Quite why the 1611 Bible doesn't call him a murderer I don't know. The word had been in existence for several centuries, and at very much the same time that the King James version was being readied for publication, the dramatis personae of Shakespeare's *Macbeth* included not merely "Three murderers," but "Other Murderers," plus the usurper king who accuses himself of murdering sleep. "Murder," in fact, is a word that runs through the play. It is the bloodiest of deeds, a foul crime, a sin against not merely the state and civil law but against Heaven. Hence, Macbeth's dreadful utterance about giving his soul, "mine eternal jewel," to Satan "the common enemy of man." (Act 3 i.)

At which point we need to bring in the first definition of crime in the *O.E.D.* to which I earlier alluded. Crime is "Sinfulness, wickedness; wrongdoing, sin." This running together of terms becomes intensely problematic once enough people decide that an act deemed sinful by religion — any religion — shouldn't be considered a crime against society. Homosexuality is an obvious case in point. And for that matter, crimes against the state may be prompted by private conscience and the commands of "natural justice." And what then? Sophocles' *Antigone* has proved of endless fascination to those who understand the irresolvable tension between those who claim to uphold the laws of the state (Creon in Sophocles' play) and those, including his son's intended wife, for whom the pull of individual conscience is stronger than such laws.

## IV

Antigone dies for her cause. Tiresias has warned Creon of the consequences of his command that she shall not bury the body of her brother, Polynices, Oedipus's contumacious son, who has warred with his equally contumacious brother, Eteocles, for the kingdom of Thebes, as a result of which their father has visited on both the curse that they should die at each other's hand. Tragic consequences flow from predetermined actions. But predetermined doesn't mean premeditated. It is this which is decisively new in the account of Cain's murder of his brother. Because murder, so the *O.E.D.* says, is "the unlawful premeditated killing of one human being by another." And in the Old Testament, the omniscient God knows what is happening. There is no hiding place. Nor was there from the Gods on Olympus, but whereas they were feckless, irrational and arbitrary in their exercise of power, the God who watches over Cain is, whatever Randolph Churchill's opinion of him may be, intended as a just God. Knowingly to go against his law is to sin.

This is why the Old Testament has so much to say about sin. Take for example, God's warning in *Ezekiel*:

"But when the righteous turneth away from his righteousness, and committeth iniquity, and doeth according to all the abominations that the wicked man doeth, shall he live? None of his righteous deeds that he hath done shall be remembered: in his trespass that he hath trespassed, and in his sin that he hath sinned, in them shall he die." (Ch. 18, verse 24.) And if anyone should be so rash as to ask how God can be confident of this, the answer is because, as Job accepts, God sees all. For Job, such acceptance is also protest: "Is it good that thou shouldst oppress .... That thou inquirest after mine iniquity, And searchest after my sin, Although thou knowest that I am not wicked, And there is none that can deliver out of thine hand?" (*Job*, Ch. 10, verses 3–7.) But Job finally comes to acknowledge that the all-knowing God is also beyond human comprehension. ("Doth the hawk fly south by thy wisdom?") Sin is then "the purposeful disobedience of a creature to the known will of God."

Like Job, Macbeth knows that he can't escape God's knowledge of the "deep damnation" of Duncan's "taking off." His faults "fly up to heaven." According to St Paul, nobody can escape God's universal law. Even the gentiles "do by nature the things of the law, these, having no law, are a law unto themselves; in that they shew the work of the law written in their hearts, their conscience bearing witness therewith, and their thoughts one with another accusing or else excusing them..." (*Romans*, Ch. 2, verses 14–15.) God, who sees into men's hearts — so Matthew reports Jesus as saying — is therefore the first and greatest detective. He not only knows what men do, he knows what they are planning to do. There is no mean street he cannot and will not go down, and no-one can escape his judgement.

## V

But by the 19th century it was becoming evident that there were mean streets aplenty in which God's law did not run. And not merely mean streets. This is not the place to discuss the reasons for Robert Peel's creation of the modern police force. I do, however, think it relevant to quote the following:

> I want to suppose a certain SHADOW, which may go into any place ... and be in all homes, and all nooks and corners, and be supposed to be cognisant of everything, and go everywhere, without the least difficulty ... a kind of semi-omniscient, omnipresent, intangible creature ... I want him to issue his warnings from time to time, that he is going to fall on such and such a subject; or to expose such and such a piece of humbug... I want him to loom as a Fanciful Shadow all over London.

This is Dickens, writing to his friend, John Forster, in 1849, to tell him of his plans for a journal, *Household Words*, which will include, among "essays, reviews, letters, theatrical criticisms, &c. &c., as amusing as possible," what nowadays would be called investigative journalism, fearless in its determination to expose corruption in high as well as low places. But it is, famously, Inspector Bucket who in *Bleak House* plunges into slums and rookeries, who is the embodiment of the Shadow, who is led unerringly to the murderer of Mr Tulkinghorn, and who in the process becomes, as it were, God's agent.

There is a coda to this. While I was drafting this essay on The First Murderer I happened to mention it to my son. The previous week, he told me, he and his wife had been invited to look at state secondary schools in their catchment area, to one of which their elder daughter would be transferring next year. Other parents were invited to make the tour of inspection and at one of the schools a parent asked the head teacher about bullying. Was there much of it and if so how did the school cope? "In the past," the head teacher said, "pupils were perhaps deterred by the thought that God could see them misbehave. Now we have CCTV."

# Portland
## *Paul Barker*

*Portland, wrote Hardy, hunches out into the Channel
like a snail: the perfect place for a prison.*

On the day I was on the winding road up to the high stone gate of the Verne prison on Portland, the Dorset constabulary were appealing for John Hannan, an Irish prisoner who had absconded from Verne, to give himself up. "If you read this," the local police magazine editorialised, "please write in. We would love to hear from you."

The snag is that Mr Hannan escaped 42 years ago, 30 days into his 21-month sentence. The governor at the Verne said, very reasonably: "For all I know he could be sitting in a pub in Ireland with a pint of Guinness."

John Hannan would be 64 now, if he is alive at all. The chances of a friendly phone call or letter — to recall old times at Verne in the 1950s, or to say he is catching the next boat back — seem minuscule.

The Portland prisons have always specialised in Irish prisoners, meaning Fenians. But Hannan was a car thief. Verne prison lies inside an old military citadel. Even from the outside, I feel oppressed by its Piranesian walls, built with convict labour high above the snot-green sea. Once you got out of here, you would somehow have to sneak across the narrow causeway from the Isle and on to the Dorset mainland. I admire Hannan's ingenuity.

Portland is one of the most extraordinary places I have ever been in. Thomas Hardy noted that it hunches out into the English Channel like a snail. He wrote one of his strangest (and least-read) novels about the Isle and its inbred, incestuous world. I have the Penguin of this novel, *The Well-Beloved*, in my jacket pocket as I cross the causeway, next to the high pebble bank of Chesil Beach.

(Portland goes in for stunning displays of geology.) The only other people going my way are birdwatchers with backpacks and binoculars. The Isle is a stopping-off point for nearly every British migratory bird — and some birds that just get lost (bee-eaters, phalaropes, hoopoes).

It remains a secret place, though not quite in the sense it was in Hardy's day. (Older churchyards are packed with cohorts of Combens, Lanos, Pearces, Elliotts and Stones, all merrily intermarried.) Today you can't turn round without bumping into a defence establishment. The Admiralty's underwater weapons research centre at Portland hosted a celebrated cold-war spy case. Secrets, stolen by a local couple, were ferried out to Moscow by the Krogers and Gordon Lonsdale. Now you can rarely dodge the sight of barbed wire or closed-circuit television.

It was the navy, and its attendant bureaucrats, who started to dilute Portland's old population and its old habits. One of these, chronicled by Hardy, was that betrothed couples always had sex. If the woman got pregnant, they were meant for each other, and they married. If not, then not. Marie Stopes bought an old lighthouse here as a summer-house. (Hardy came to stay.) Portland was a good place for contraceptive propaganda. Or perhaps her motives were different. She said she conceived her only child at the lighthouse. (And, yes, it does look like a stubby phallus.)

The Isle's inhabitants now are mainly naval, or quarrymen digging out the world-famous stone, or convicts, or their keepers. Convicts were first brought here to do forced labour, ten hours a day, on the great breakwaters of the naval harbour. I walk over a worn trig mark in the pavement next to Portland's oldest prison. It is now a euphemistic "Young Offenders' Institution"; older prisoners are at Verne. The trig stone has the War Department broad arrow on it, which the first convicts always wore, and still wear in children's comics.

The third and newest prison at Portland was imported by Michael Howard. Jack Straw attacked the idea; in office he accepted it. It is a prison ship, brought over ready-made from America.

But where is it? Trying to find this latter-day version of Magwitch's hulk, I start at the naval harbour. It is empty, except for a flotilla of white-sailed leisure dinghies; I assume it is a race. The helicopters of the coastguard rescue service doze at the water's edge, like red-and-white insects. There are fences and security men everywhere. Behind me are the Admiralty's blank brown office blocks.

I go up the winding shore road. A taxi passes, with a flinty blonde in the back, on her way up to visiting hours at the Verne. I turn off into a poverty-stricken council estate. People huddle from the wind in cheap parkas. Most of the cars are Ladas. Only one tenant seems to have gone for right-to-buy. The garden is packed with cement ornaments. I step round the dog shit on a muddy path, and go over to the cliff edge. Now I can see fragments of Mulberry harbour, a BT ship — and the floating prison.

It looks like a grey crate, resting on the water. It is so box-like I am amazed that it is seaworthy. It has five rows of barred windows on each side. There is no sign of movement. It couldn't be more out of sight and out of mind. Another Portland secret.

# Scrappin' wi' Scouse
## *John Stuart Clark*

It was a Saturday, furniture and bric-à-brac day down at Meadow Lane cattle market, and the auction room was rammed. Most of the punters were landlords and ladies looking to fit out student lets on the cheap. The dealers had cornered the good stuff the evening before, viewing night, but the damp shed next to the sheep pens remained the best place in town to collar a bargain. He must have really muscled through the congealed bodies behind me.

'Clarkie,' he hissed, squeezing my arm, 'y'got sixty quid?'

The waft of Park Drives and stale sweat, the rasping voice and stubby tattooed paw had to belong to the big man. I half-turned, keeping a wary eye on bidding for a battered Victorian dresser I fancied.

'Jesus, Scouse! I have, but it's a lot of...'

'We'll double it back by t'night. Y'got it on you?'

Sixty pounds was a significant sum in 1973, but I'd recently thrown in the towel on a fledgling career as a film lecturer and was relatively flush. It wasn't that the job had no prospects — there were less than ten of us in the country back then — but I'd gone from graduate to academic in the blink of a degree ceremony and, two years down the line, worried there was an awful lot of living that semiological critiques of Truffaut's *œuvre* weren't providing.

Within twenty minutes of handing over the cash I was the surprised owner of a bright red Ford Transit van that had evidently earned its stripes hauling something disgustingly black and greasy. Scouse assured me the paperwork would eventually materialise. I never did get to meet the previous owner and, eighteen months later, we were pulled by coppers who informed us it was a stolen vehicle.

Saturday evening we sat in The Alma pub counting our takings. Ferrying furniture from auction room to various addresses in Radford, St. Ann's and Hyson Green, prime territories for Rachmanesque landlords, we had cleared £200. I took my half of the profit and handed Scouse the keys to the Tranny. That's when he told me he couldn't drive, had never mastered it, and we were now partners. By the time the partnership dissolved, I had learned more about urban survival than a lifetime in higher education could teach, and the love I felt for the old rascal was greater than for my real father.

Scouse was a bear of a man, overweight, ungainly, bearded like Santa and prone to going weeks without taking a bath. His clothes came from jumble sales, and it wasn't often he encumbered his boots with laces, possibly a hangover from his years banged up. Socks and underwear were optional extras, though he was fond of string vests, the less string the better. A decade or so before his time, he could have been the model for Rab C. Nesbitt, down to the fags and booze and utter disdain for what you and I call 'honest employment'. Despite his name, you had to listen hard to pick up the Liverpudlian beneath the washed gravel of PDs and Home Ales. His punch-bag face and rolling limp belied a man well-acquainted with hard knocks. He was somewhere in his early fifties going on late sixties.

I first came across him breaking into an empty two-up two-down on Maples Street, in one of the rougher necks of the city. As he explained it, by entering through the window, we weren't technically breaking in. Kicking down the door was clearly illegal, but shimmying the window latch and staking a claim to occupancy somehow bestowed squatters' rights. Never did get my head round that, but I was only there in the hope of satisfying an unrequited lust for one of the three women Scouse was helping to house.

In the early Seventies, the north of our city was a hotbed of housing disputes and strikes in the rag trade, both supported by the Claimants Union in whatever way furthered their 'Revolution'. In theory, everybody who received state benefits was an unsigned-up member of the union, but the core activists were a handful of highly educated and wilfully unemployed Lefties living in squats around Forest Road in variations on a theme of collective. How Scouse got involved with them isn't clear, except he was an inveterate claimant, had a bed in one of the collectives and was a useful man to have around, despite being twice their age. While the articulate banged on about 'organising the proletariat' in interminable 'house meetings', Scouse walked the streets scoping properties ripe for squatting.

Though still trying to turn students onto the dark wonders of German Expressionist Cinema, I brushed against this mob, even helped a few aggrieved tenants lever their just desserts out of the Social, but Scouse and myself were barely on nodding terms until the big man grabbed my arm. For the next four years he was to ride shotgun while I took the reins, steering our battered Tranny through the back streets and knockings of Greater Nottingham, searching for anything that would earn us a crust. Today we might be called 'free-range recyclers'. Scouse called us 'tatters' or 'scrappers', sometimes 'pikeys'. Whatever we were, it was a world apart from any I knew existed.

A flavour of our working day would be poking round the factory yards of the spinning mills tucked away in Long Eaton, west of the city. We never possessed a street map, but by instinct or scent of moolah, Scouse knew exactly where to turn, when and how slowly to drive by to afford a good shufty at the piles of scrap, empty barrels and bins of rags dumped inside the perimeter. If he saw something sweet, we'd pull over to discuss our approach, what to offer, where to off-load and, in some cases, how the hell to jam the haul in or on the Tranny. When we made our pitch, Scouse did all the talking. He had a patter today's spin-doctors would die for.

Some pickings, like barrels, we had to fork out for, payola that either went to the works' tea-kitty or disappeared into the yard manager's pocket. Since every tatter on the road was after steel barrels, we had to better the deal the manager already received, preferably boosting our offer with services rendered rather than extra cash. We'd clean up the yard, sort out the swarf, take away rubbish (fly-tipped at the first opportunity), grim tasks that made our hands bleed but were a license to rummage deeper and wider round the site. Invariably this reaped a harvest of nice-little-earners like wheel rims or lead piping, discreetly squirrelled into the van without consent.

Scrap didn't fetch much of a price in those days, unless it was non-ferrous. A Tranny full of steel barely earned us thirty notes, but we took knackered machines and vehicle parts on the same pretext of getting to the real earners. We travelled with sledgehammer, crowbar and rope, and smashed up lathes and looms on site, separating the ally and zinc from cast and steel for a better deal at the merchants. Copper cabling guaranteed good money, though we had to burn off the sheaves, a toxic rubber bonfire lit on the waste ground of a gravel quarry adjacent to the chintzy suburb of Attenborough that has since become a nature reserve. Rags were a pain in the arse — the shape of the bins wasted valuable space in the back of the Tranny — but you could get decent dosh if you knew where to go and what to do. And Scouse did.

At best, we could only hit the factories once a month. There simply wasn't the turnover in the sluggish Seventies, but people always needed work on their cars. (Introduced incrementally in the 1960s, the MOT test bit hard in the 1970s.) In the course of a day trawling every small garage in a target zone like Radford or Bulwell, we could generally scrounge an acceptable haul of bent fenders, mashed gearboxes, dead dynamos and spent batteries. Now and again we scored a complete vehicle, towing it to some quiet dead-end for dismembering before heading off to Attenborough to torch the seats. The mess of shattered glass and plastic we left on residential streets now shames me, and I have no idea how we managed to heave the flattened wreck onto the Tranny's roof. With it precariously attached by a loose bandage of rope, our drives through the city centre attracted no shortage of attention, from everybody except the cops.

Duff starter motors and aluminium number plates required extra graft to release their earning potential. Within a year we had a bench and vice set up in Scouse's bedroom, where we stripped and separated ferrous from non. For all their gestures of 'solidarity with the working classes', the collective was less than solid with the reek of oil and pounding of lump hammers. The gloves came off when we trundled in two huge gas cylinders to fuel an oxyacetylene burner. A flurry of 'house meetings' concluded the cutting torch was a tool too far. Scouse concluded it was suck it or lose him. Since he was now 'The Scrounger' (James Garner's role in *The Great Escape*) everybody wanted living in *their* collective, game over.

Small garages and factory units became our bread 'n' butter. By segmenting the city and prowling every street, we gradually built regular rounds. Every new score was one lost by some other bunch of tatters. We made enemies, but that went with the territory. The difficulty was hanging on to your round. What ensured our fickle suppliers wouldn't cave in to better offers was our entertainment value. Next to Scouse, I was plainly a fish out of water and downright pathetic at humping. I became the butt of pranks and jokes stored up and rehearsed during the week, joshing that reached a peak when the driver's sliding door developed a will of its own, clattering to the ground whenever I stopped or started, or even drove. Entire workforces would down tools, line up and wait for us to pull away. By year three, we were travelling with the damn door slung in the back, with nothing between me and the wind but my sleeve. Several times we weighed it in by mistake.

But we also built up a unique knowledge of the most productive areas of Nottingham, and where there's muck there really is money, or at least money to be saved. The more industrial an area, the more fringe benefits were to be found 'lying around'. Middle-class manors like West Bridgford and Beeston were too tight to bother with — anything snot-gobblers hossed out had to be paid for — but the inner city provided rich pickings. Like a Geiger counter continually beeping, Scouse's nose continually twitched, swinging into over-drive when it caught a whiff of something juicy behind a printing works, on an allotment, beside a corner shop, outside a warehouse, down a ginnel. We snaffled tea urns, kitchen-units, Wilton carpets, one-arm bandits, lawnmowers, Roneo machines, filing cabinets — all manner of goodies probably awaiting collection by some soon-to-be-miffed second-hand dealer. We always had space for a serviceable sofa or fridge, and there was always a squat or impoverished family we knew would be grateful. And we had a van, a bit of a rarity among city activists, so if somebody or something needed shifting, we were y'boys.

A case in point was the newfangled adventure playground residents in the Arboretum area were trying to get off the ground. Long before community workers stuck their snouts into neighbourhood movements and neutralised them, communities got it together and did constructive things for themselves. We were asked to keep an eye out for sturdy lengths of timber, the main pillars for a wooden shambles children could range over. We found them beside the tracks in Stapleford and 'liberated' them from British Rail, who clearly had no use for spanking new sleepers. As Scouse always put it, they were just 'lying around', albeit on private property.

In a similar way, the Nottingham City Museums Service (or whatever they've been rebranded) benefited from our flexible interpretation of property laws. Several times Scouse landed us choice house clearance jobs, mainly in periphery villages where our reputation had yet to travel. One such was Gamston Hall, a dilapidated tower of a building with farmhouse and barns attached. Mothballed in the barns were a couple of Triumph Mayflowers from the 1950s Scouse was itching to get his hands on, but 'lying around' I spotted a number of wooden ice makers, three-legged stools, and cheese and butter churns from a bygone era. All are still on display in the Museum of Nottingham Life, 'liberated' and donated by Anonymous. We didn't get the Mayflowers, mostly because we had nowhere to store them.

Of course, sometimes our light fingers got burned, though never by a run-in with the law (Scouse was far too canny and had the innocent dimwit down to perfection). The comeuppance that sticks with me wreaked its revenge a year or so after our partnership dissolved. I had moved on to 'honest employment' with a community arts group newly ensconced in the old General Dispensary in Hyson Green. Originally a doctor's surgery, the stern Edwardian building stood empty for years and had been a sitting duck for metal strippers. The arties froze in there during summer, and in winter we huddled an inch from an industrial fan heater, cursing the toe-rags who ripped out the boiler and cast piping that once made the surgery toasty for patients to strip off in. Needless to say, I mentioned nothing about my past life or that the haul paid handsomely.

If our foraging was in the twilight zone of legal trading, getting shot of our loads placed us bang in the middle of dealers who were not averse to inflicting a casual kneecapping. A few of the scrap merchants played it pretty straight, notably McIntyre's on Harriman's Lane, the largest yard in town, but most were far from kosher about the prices they paid and what they'd take. Scouse recounted unrepeatable stories about the criminal proclivities of the brothers who owned Nottingham Scrap

Metal, for example, and drummed it in that we really didn't want to cross the Neanderthal who ran Haydn Scrap. The name of the game was to keep them all chipper by trading with each at least once a month, and not to quibble about the payout. There were ways to exploit their surfeit of brawn over brains, Scouse explained.

All scrap and waste material deals are made on weight. The rag merchants weighed your bins when you arrived, despatched you into their yard to dump the contents, then weighed them empty when you left. Backing up the Tranny with the rear hidden from the office, we could surreptitiously remove lumps of cast iron buried beneath the rags for the weigh-in, thus doubling our earnings at the weigh-out. There were two entrances at the old power station on Queen's Drive, but you weighed in scrap at one, drove out, then into the other to off-load. Since the second gate wasn't visible from the weighbridge, Scouse had me driving hell-for-leather round to the ever-efficient McIntyre's, where we weighed in, off-loaded and got paid, before screaming back empty to the power station for a second payout. With scrap, they weighed the whole vehicle, so it made financial sense to always have a heap of mud and stone secreted in the back, slyly brushed out at the off-load. And a favourite trick with wrecked cars was to top up the tanks with water or fill them with sand (neither of which dispelled the fumes), rather than remove the tanks altogether, as the merchants required. This literally backfired when McIntyre's invested in a gargantuan conveyor belt that crushed and separated and sorted the metals before incinerating the upholstery. We were the first to blow it to pieces, but pointed the finger at 'gyppos' from Newark who obliged by looking guilty.

Nobody on the scrap liked Gypsies, which was odd, given the number of tatters Scouse knew for a fact had Romany in them. He fraternised with the competition at the Irish Centre on Wilford Street, boozing and bragging sessions I wasn't a part of, even when present. They fizzled out when it became obvious we were actually hobnobbing with more IRA sympathisers and fugitives than was healthy in the year Lord Mountbatten got blown to bits. But Scouse's own mongrel bloodline, apparently laced with Pavee, served us well on the few occasions we had dealings with the king tatters up in Tinsley, Sheffield.

We regularly cleared the Sawley yard of Carters the drink manufacturers, famous for their Horehound Beer, but on this visit found a redundant and massive stainless steel steriliser for disposal, way too big and much too valuable for Tranny tatters like us. Pounding straight up to Sheffield before Nottingham's big boys whipped it from under us, Scouse directed me to two rows of terrace houses standing proud of a demolished estate signed for redevelopment. (Apparently the king tatters had bought the whole street and weren't budging.) Depositing me in one of the homes to suffer steri tea and admire the family's remarkable collection of all things brass, he disappeared, returning an hour later with a big grin on his face and a hessian sack of used tenners in his mit. On the journey back, he revealed we were also proud owners of four greyhounds, two horses and a *vardo* (traditional Gypsy caravan). I haven't a clue what became of them, and the steriliser was never mentioned again, but we were on Jameson's for the rest of the year.

Friday evenings were usually spent touring the pubs of Radford, The Meadows and St. Ann's, where codgers and scallywags hunched over pints, puffing and nattering, and checking their polythene bags were still at their feet. We arrived with similar bags of pewter vases, brass candlesticks, vintage carriage clocks — anything crusty we reckoned would make a tasty trade. Having surveyed the bar, checking for scumbags who held a grudge against us, Scouse worked the tables while I bought the beers and watched his back. By the end of the night, plaggy bags had changed hands any number of times in any number of pubs like some citywide cup-and-ball trick. Our final tallies never failed to surprise and delight me. Aside from cash and a little something for somebody one of us had in mind, there would be ham hocks, portable TVs, caterer's packs of bacon and bangers, ghetto blasters, boxes of vegetables, cartons of fags, sportswear, venison, bicycle parts nicked from the Raleigh — you name it, we handled it. And almost all our Friday booty, including the money, went through the Claimants Union or various tenants groups to deserving causes. Scouse never forgot where he laid his head at night.

They were four strange, exciting years that appealed to the cowboy in me, but they took their toll. No matter how often I bathed, I could never expunge the stench of petrol, oil, sweat and burnt rubber, a gut-heaving cocktail that put paid to any romance coming my way. My backbone had welded into a discernible stoop, my shins were scraped raw by sheets of metal slipping out of hand, and my palms looked like trench warfare had been waged on them. Scouse's hands became a mess of small tectonic plates that crackled as they nudged against each other when he flexed, and his Love and Hate finger tattoos had disappeared beneath a layer of ingrained oil and muck. By the third year, we had restricted our tatting to autumn through spring. We spent the summer recovering, basking in the glow of undeclared earnings that made the Social go a lot further and the sun feel a lot warmer. Certainly, it was the winter months that did the damage — cold steel handled on a freezing day strips skin, and nobody used gloves in those days — but we figured the savings we made on heating by being out and about in the Tranny more than compensated. There was also the seasonal incentive that our 'comrades' in the collective spent their winters dossing around the house, whinging about the slow pace of 'Revolution'.

Our partnership ended shortly after Tranny gave up the ghost. It had served us, the squatters, the Lefties and various community and tenants groups well, incredibly well, considering the abuse heaped upon it. The bodywork suffered that many bangs and scrapes and dousings in gunk, you would never have known the poor sod was once a telephone box red. Barely an original mechanical part remained by the time we all spluttered reluctantly towards the final weigh-in, its own. Scouse and myself upgraded to a more practical diesel pick-up, then a totally impractical GPO crew-wagon, but scrapping wasn't the same without Tranny to entertain us.

I lived in the same collective as Scouse for much of our partnership and beyond, but in all our years together I learned precious little about the man behind the Santa beard (though a lot more than anybody else in Nottingham). His real name was William Holloway, somewhat ironic for a bloke who'd done time in every prison in England *except* Holloway, the women's prison. From what I could discern, his crimes amounted to multiples of petty theft, disorderly conduct, vagrancy and beating the crap out of coppers during arrest. Apparently, the villainy started at the end of World War II when he went AWOL from somewhere in Europe, possibly Paris, but I suspect Scouse was always on the wrong side of laws he considered bollocks and authority he consider pitiful. I learned he'd been a steel erector, a fairground pugilist and tarmac navvy, travelling around the country with gangs of equally restless demobbed squaddies. And I learned he had a daughter somewhere, and was desperately lonely. He craved female companionship and a relationship deeper than those he had with the women in our circle, who basically saw him as a lovable old eccentric.

Scouse eventually moved down to Bristol, latterly attaching himself to a handful of young families squatting the spacious Old Rectory in Chew Magna, south of the city, a Grade II listed former convalescent home. I visited with some trepidation, but was delighted to find my old mucker happily lodged in his own ground floor flat, surrounded by all the children and love he could have wished for in his closing years. When he lost his mobility, the collective knocked out a wall and fitted bay windows that opened onto the garden where the kids played. Beside his bed, a colourful portrait by one of the squatters depicted the big man like a comfy armchair, with the artist's son sat on his lap cushioned in his great beard. Top right, a line drawing showed the back of a little Scouse flying away on wings, a bindle stick slung over his left shoulder.

When his hammered body finally gave out, I took a trip down Memory Lane to McIntyre's non-ferrous shed, to pass the sad news onto Popeye, one of Scouse's old cellmates and a poacher-turned-gamekeeper. Beside the skips of copper, zinc and ally, we had a quiet weep. To my eternal regret, I never attended his funeral. It would have been too painful.

# Convicted Out of His Own Mouth? How Forensic Linguistics Cleared Derek Bentley's Name
*Danuta Reah*

*I'm Jack.*
*I see you are still having no luck catching me...*

(Opening of a hoax tape recording sent to detectives investigating the Yorkshire Ripper murders).

In 1979, at the height of the Yorkshire Ripper killings, a tape was sent to the chief investigating officer. This voice, with its chilling message, was analysed by linguists at the University of Leeds who pinpointed the speaker as coming from the former pit village of Castletown, Sunderland. This result was not helpful to the case as the tape was a hoax. However the findings were very accurate. When the hoaxer was identified and arrested in 2005, he was a man who had lived his whole life within walking distance of the area the linguists had identified. This was probably the first time that the science of forensic linguistics came to public attention.

Forensic linguistics is the study of language and the law. Its remit ranges from legal language and courtroom discourse, to linguistic analysis of spoken and written texts including disputed statements and confessions.

Linguists identify language as falling into a series of varieties and registers. Each variety will have its own characteristic features — the choice of vocabulary, the sound or look of the language, the structures typically used. These varieties can range from massive areas such as the language of the law, to the smallest: the language of an individual, that person's idiolect. Idiolect can tell you a lot about where a person comes from (as in the case of the hoax Ripper tape), it can indicate their age, their social or cultural group, their gender. TV crime drama will sometimes use this. 'Can we get a voice print?' a detective will say, and bingo, the wizards in the lab come up with an identification. 'As if,' would be the response of most forensic linguists. Linguistic 'fingerprinting' is a long way off, if it is possible at all.

So what can the forensic linguist bring to an investigation?

Language is a complex human artefact — one we all take for granted and use with casual expertise. It's relatively easy to understand why two people will recognise the meaning of the word 'chair' or the word 'dog' though their individual interpretations may vary widely. A chair is a chair is a chair, but is a dog a loving, loyal friend, or a dirty, dangerous nuisance?

Again, it's relatively easy to understand why someone will probably react appropriately to the words 'Look at that.' Say 'Look at that' to someone, point, and they will probably look in the direction you are indicating. But 'that' is a word that needs a context. Without the context, it can render an utterance meaningless. What does 'Look at that' mean if it's written on a note put through your letter box? In this case, it may mean something odd, strange and maybe slightly threatening. Context creates meaning. Context is all.

Speakers also understand nuances and the coded meaning that social and cultural factors impose on language. We know at once, if someone says 'The dog got run over,' that they are talking about a specific dog. The exchange that follows this will be very different from the one that follows 'A dog got run over.' How is it that a native speaker of British English will, in certain circumstances, understand the comment 'Did someone leave the door open?' as a request, or even an instruction, to close the door?

The complexities of language, the importance of context, the problems of analysis and usually the sparsity of data mean that a voice, or a written text, can seldom be attributed beyond all doubt to a specific speaker or writer. However, the forensic linguist can identify patterns, anomalies and possibilities. These can be compelling when the number of possible authors is small, and can be sufficient to provide proof in court. Today, also, the existence of language corpora, such as the COBUILD corpus, huge collections of spoken and written language that can be analysed electronically, provide the forensic linguist with the scientific support needed to speak with confidence about the characteristics of specific varieties and registers.

## Forensic linguistics in action: the Derek Bentley case

In 1953, in a notorious miscarriage of justice, Derek Bentley, 19, was hanged for the murder of a police constable, Sidney Miles. He was convicted in court on the basis of police evidence and a confession. The conviction was controversial for many reasons.

Bentley had been diagnosed on several occasions prior to the crime as having a developmental disorder. He was barely literate and had an IQ of 77. He was not carrying a gun. He was already in the hands of the police before his fellow accused, Christopher Craig, fired any shots. Bentley was accused of encouraging Christopher Craig to shoot, allegedly shouting 'Let him have it, Chris,' as he was trying to evade the police constable who had taken him into custody. The utterance is ambiguous. The police always claimed Bentley meant, 'Shoot him,' but in this context, what does 'it' refer to? Both Craig and Bentley denied that the words had ever been spoken.

Bentley also claimed he had no knowledge that Craig was carrying a gun, and his confession was always disputed. Bentley himself claimed the document was not what police said it was.

After his death, his family campaigned for decades to get his conviction overturned

In 1998, when the case went back yet again to the Court of Appeal, forensic linguist Professor Malcolm Coulthard analysed the confession. Rules of evidence at the time of Bentley's arrest said that records of interviews should contain both questions and responses. If an accused person chose to make a statement or confession and it was written down by the interviewing police, then the police should not ask substantive questions. Bentley's confession had been presented to the court as a 'verbatim record of dictated monologue,' that is, Bentley's own words, unprompted by police questions or interventions. This was attested under oath by three police officers.

At Bentley's trial, linguistic nuances in the confession were used to support the prosecution contention that Bentley knew Craig was carrying a gun. Confessions tend to take the form of a narrative. In any personal narrative, the narrator will talk about what happened, and possibly what he/she knew or believed. It's rare for narrators to be explicit about what did *not* happen or what the narrator did *not* know. As Coulthard says, 'There is after all an infinite number of things that did not happen and thus the teller needs to have some special justification for reporting any of them to the listener.' (Coulthard and Johnson 2007, p163)

A narrator might deny things that a listener may infer from a narrative. A child might say 'Mum put the cakes on the table. I didn't eat any of them.' The child is unlikely to say 'Mum put the cakes on the table. She didn't say anything. I didn't eat any,' unless a question on the lines of 'Did she tell you not to touch them?' had been asked.

Throughout Bentley's narrative, he denies things the listener might infer from what he says, but he also denies things the listener would have no reason to infer. A key sentence from the trial 'I didn't know he was going to use the gun' occurs in this context:

> When we came to the place where you found me, Chris looked in the window. There was a little iron gate at the side. Chris then jumped over and I followed. Chris then climbed up the drainpipe to the roof and I followed. Up to then Chris had not said anything. We both got out on to the flat roof at the top. Then someone in a garden on the opposite side shone a torch up towards us. Chris said: 'It's a copper, hide behind here.' We hid behind a shelter arrangement on the roof. We were there waiting for about ten minutes. *I did not know he was going to use the gun.* A plain clothes man climbed up the drainpipe and on to the roof. The man said 'I am a police officer — the place is surrounded'.

The highlighted sentence is the first reference in the statement to the gun Craig was carrying. The judge, in his summing up said that if Bentley genuinely had not known Craig had a gun, he would have said '*a* gun,' not '*the* gun,' and he would not have mentioned it in his narrative at that point. This meant that his denials later in the narrative, where he said he did not know Craig had a gun, (here, the phrase 'a gun' was used, as would be expected if this was new information within the narrative) were unreliable. Bentley knew Craig had a gun and was therefore as culpable as Craig who fired the shot.

Ironically, Christopher Craig at 16 was too young to be hanged, and was released from prison on parole 10 years later. He always supported Bentley's version of events.

Coulthard demonstrated in his analysis that several features of Bentley's statement gave a clear indication that he was being prompted by questions. These included denials in his narrative confession where there was no reason for the listener to have made an inference.

For example:
— *Chris then climbed up the drainpipe to the roof and I followed.*

— Up to then **Chris had not said anything**.
— *We both got out on to the flat roof at the top.*

There is no relevance to this comment. It is out of place in the narrative as Bentley does not mention talking himself, Craig talking once they got onto the roof, or anyone else talking at this time.

— *[The policeman] caught hold of me and as we walked away Chris fired.*
— **There was nobody else there at the time.**
— *The policeman and I then went round a corner by a door.*

And crucially

— *We hid behind a shelter arrangement on the roof.*
— *We were there waiting for about ten minutes.*
— **I did not know he was going to use the gun.**

Again, there is no narrative relevance to these denials. Who said there was anyone else there? Who said Bentley knew about the gun? No one, in the context of the confession. But did someone ask, and did Bentley respond to their question?

Further support to the contention that the confession was not what it was claimed to be, a verbatim recording of Bentley's unsolicited words, is the occurrence throughout of the post-positioned 'then', 'I then,' rather than 'then I.' Analysis of language corpora demonstrated how anomalous this was in a statement apparently dictated verbatim to the police.

In the COBUILD corpus, a 2.5 billion word collection of contemporary English, an analysis of the most frequently used words shows 'then' as the 58th most frequent word in spoken English, and the 85th most frequently used word in the corpus overall. In Derek Bentley's statement, it is the 8th most frequently used word. It is also used in a very distinctive way — the post-positioned 'then' — a feature that occurs only once every 165,000 words in COBUILD. It is found far more frequently in police statements but almost never in the register of ordinary witness statements. Coulthard's evidence showed that Bentley's 'verbatim record of dictated monologue,' sworn to be such in court by three police officers, was a compilation of question and answer. Once the confession is seen in this light, the anomalies vanish. It no longer demonstrates that Bentley knew Craig was carrying a gun. He was simply responding to questions asked him by police officers, questions that were not recorded, and were denied in court.

The forensic linguistic evidence, along with other evidence led to Derek Bentley's conviction being quashed in 1998. This was too late for Bentley's sister Iris, who had campaigned tirelessly for his conviction to be overturned who had died a year earlier, forty-four years after her brother had been hanged.

## References

Coulthard, M. (2005) The Linguist as Expert Witness, *Linguistics and the Human Sciences,* 1, i, 39-58

Coulthard, M. and Johnson, A., 2007, *An Introduction to Forensic Linguistics: Language in Evidence*, Routledge, London

# The Kerry Babies Case: a Crime Against Women
## *Deirdre O'Byrne*

It was a warm night in mid-1985. I was walking home, taking a shortcut through the grounds of a hospital. Some lads were having a smoke on a seat near Our Lady's grotto. One of them called out, 'Hey, look! She's moving!'. I was amused, but kept my head down and carried on walking, ignoring him and his chuckling pals. We all knew what he meant: it was the Summer of the Moving Statues (more about that later), and in the moonlight, my long, pale cotton dress somewhat resembled Mary's robes. It has stayed with me, that innocuous non-event, perhaps because it has in retrospect assumed a symbolic meaning. I was in my late twenties, not afraid to walk home alone after dark, but wary of joining in openly with the lads' joke. I'd learned the code of behaviour — euphemistically: 'Don't encourage them' — but then, I'd had to. All around me were stories of what happened to Irish women who ignored the code: Ann Lovett, found dead with her newborn baby in a field; Eileen Flynn, a schoolteacher, sacked from her job when she became pregnant; Joanne Hayes, vilified for her affair with a married man. The women were all young; Flynn and Hayes were in their twenties, and Lovett was only fifteen. Journalist Nell McCafferty wrote that:

> The nineteen-eighties will go down in history as a lousy decade for Irishwomen. During what became known as 'the amendment years', church and state fought for control of our bodies and our destiny. The Catholic church won handily, and the Irish Constitution contains written prohibitions against abortion and divorce. Debate on all these matters spilled over into all areas of the female condition, widening the scope for an unprecedented torrent of abuse and insult.

Of these abusive torrents, the most vicious was against Joanne Hayes, in what became known as The Kerry Babies Case. It began with the discovery of a baby's body, subsequently referred to as 'the Cahirciveen baby', on a beach near Cahirciveen in April 1984. Garda (police) enquiries turned up the name of Joanne Hayes from Abbeydorney, who had been pregnant, but no longer was, with no baby in evidence. A local hospital revealed that Joanne had checked in saying she'd had a miscarriage, though tests showed that she had brought a baby to full term. The Hayes family were brought in to Tralee Garda Station for questioning. Joanne repeatedly said she had borne a baby (later referred to as 'the Abbeydorney baby') which had died, that she had hidden its body on the family farm, and offered to show the Gardaí where it was. They apparently didn't believe her. After several hours, Joanne and her family signed statements saying a baby had been born on the farm, stabbed by Joanne, and brought by her siblings to the coast and dumped in the sea. There is no evidence that Joanne or her family ever travelled to the coast or dumped any baby in the sea other than this confession, later retracted.

The Gardaí case subsequently unravelled. Blood tests revealed that the Cahirciveen baby could not have been the child of Joanne and Jer Locke, the married man with whom she'd been having an affair. Joanne's baby, 'the Abbeydorney baby', was indeed found on the farm, where she said it was, and charges were dropped against the Hayes family. The story might have ended there had not journalists got hold of it. Their report caused a public outcry. The Hayes family were interviewed again, and alleged that they were bullied into making false statements. A Tribunal ensued to enquire into the case. It lasted from December 1984 to June the following year.

While the Tribunal was ostensibly set up to examine the conduct of the Gardaí, what actually happened was a public excoriation of Joanne Hayes and her sexual behaviour. She'd had an affair with a married man, and become pregnant three times by him. She'd had one miscarriage, a daughter Yvonne lived, and the third child, 'the Abbeydorney baby', a boy, was born on 13 April 1984. When Yvonne was born, Joanne believed that her lover would leave his wife for her, whereas by the time she'd become pregnant for the third time, she no longer held that illusion. She had discovered that Locke's wife was also pregnant, and the affair had come to an end. Joanne, heartbroken and ashamed, hadn't discussed her latest pregnancy with her family. She told the Gardaí that she'd had the baby outside, that it had died and she had buried it on the Abbeydorney family farm without mentioning it to her mother, sister or brothers. This reticent family were hardly to know that intimate details of their life were about to be made public in the most painful and humiliating way.

Throughout the Tribunal, Gardaí continued to deny the Hayes's allegations that they had been coerced into falsehoods, despite the fact that the statements given by the family differed in crucial details, including who was in the car when the alleged journey to the coast had been taken. Joanne said the Gardaí were 'roaring and shouting' at her during questioning, threatening that the farm would be sold and her daughter Yvonne put into care. Her siblings gave similar details of intimidation and harassment. In an effort to besmirch Joanne's reputation and brand her as untrustworthy, the most intimate details of her behaviour were aired at the Tribunal. She was in tears on several occasions, and once was physically sick outside the courtroom. So, after an episode in which she and her family were bullied in the privacy of a Garda station, the judiciary sought to exonerate its officers by more prolonged harassment in the public arena of the Tribunal, held in the intimidating venue of Tralee Courthouse.

The Hayes's Abbeydorney neighbours protested outside the courthouse at the treatment of Joanne, and women's groups from around the country marched with placards.

When handed a submission from the Tralee women's group, on behalf of Irish women, the tribunal's presiding Judge Lynch (ironic name, that, given the lynching that Hayes endured) asked: 'What have I got to do with the women of Ireland in general? What have the women of Ireland in general got to do with this case?'. The final verdict of the Tribunal exonerated the Gardaí, dismissing their bending of the truth as 'gilding the lily', whereas the Hayes family were accused of telling 'barefaced lies'. A judicious use of language, one might say. The double standard is obvious, but double standards were no news in 1980s Ireland.

I followed the case in *The Irish Times*, which I bought every day because I had become obsessed with solving their Crosaire cryptic crossword. I became adept with practice, but then, deciphering cryptic clues was a survival strategy, especially for women. The conundrums set by Crosaire were a doddle compared to the doublethink going on at the Tribunal. The Gardaí alleged they hadn't been questioning the Hayes family over the baby at Cahirciveen, a claim the judge branded 'a load of nonsense'. In an attempt to pin the murder of the Cahirciveen baby upon Joanne, Gardaí came up with the very unlikely theory that she'd had twins by two different fathers, and that one ('the Abbeydorney baby') had been buried on the farm and the other thrown into the sea and washed up in Cahirciveen. When it was pointed out that blood tests indicated she couldn't have borne the Cahirciveen baby, they still stuck to their twins story, and alleged that one infant had been cast into the ocean but remained unfound.

Aside from this preposterous allegation, there were other moments of farce in the course of the Tribunal. In an examination of the Hayes home, a name had been noticed on a mattress: Tom Flynn. The name was repeatedly aired in the courtroom, as the suggestion was made that this mystery man might have been Joanne's other lover, and the father of the Cahirciveen baby. It transpired that a

Tom Flynn had worked in the shop which sold the mattress and had long since emigrated to the United States. In his absence, he became something of a celebrity. The regard in which Tralee locals held the Tribunal may be judged by the fact that several young men walked around town wearing t-shirts declaring 'I am Tom Flynn'. But men could afford to make jokes. Jeremiah Locke, Joanne's lover, was also called as witness at the Tribunal but he was not given as gruelling a treatment as Joanne Hayes, and unlike her, he did not become the main target of accusations of infanticide. Somewhere out there was another shadowy figure, a mystery woman who must have followed Joanne's story with terror and trepidation: the birth mother of the baby found on the beach. She remains unknown, but must have suffered agonies through the long months of Joanne's trial by media.

Rural Ireland, in my youth and that of Joanne Hayes, was a dangerous place to step down from the pedestal of idealised womanhood. We were assumed to aspire to the allotted life narrative of veiled First Communicant, Child of Mary, virgin before marriage, Catholic [married] mother. The alternative identities were also dinned into us: brazen hussy, rip, strap, hoor. Around the time of the Eileen Flynn case, I got a lift from someone I knew slightly. He introduced the topic of Eileen Flynn, recently vilified in the media. Flynn had been teaching in a school, and become pregnant by her co-habiting lover, a man who was separated from his wife (divorce was not allowed in Ireland at the time). When her pregnancy became obvious, she lost her job. In response to the driver's comment about Flynn's dismissal, I said yes, it was terrible. After a few minutes, I realised what *he* thought was 'terrible' was Eileen Flynn's status as a co-habiting, unmarried, pregnant woman, not the fact that she was sacked. He said he wouldn't want someone like *her* teaching *his* children. I'd heard a bit about this man, and gossip didn't paint him as a saint. Depending on the age of the commentator, he was known as a go-boy or a playboy. The stories may have been untrue, and you could say, as he no doubt would, that he wasn't a teacher so his private life didn't matter. I had a personal reason to be concerned with Flynn's dismissal: I was teaching children (not his, thankfully) at the time, and only too aware that my private life was perceived to be public property. It's one of the reasons I left — the job and the country.

Eileen Flynn taught English and History, but she could hardly have foreseen that she would become a significant figure in Ireland's social history, along with teenage mother Ann Lovett, found dead in a field in front of a grotto of Our Lady, with her dead newborn beside her. Grottos became the focus of much attention in the mid-80s. In Ballinspittle in County Cork, in July 1985, Our Lady's statue was observed to have moved, allegedly. When word spread, droves of tourists arrived; car-parks with toilets and phone-boxes were provided. Then mobile Marys began 'appearing' all over Ireland. People were staring at statues, willing them to wobble. Probably envious of the tidy little tourist industry which had sprung up in Ballinspittle, the populace elsewhere urged their local Lady to get a move on.

How do we account for this? In Ryan and Kirakowski's book, *Ballinspittle: Moving Statues and Faith*, they put forward theories from boredom with the long wet summer (I must have chosen the only warm dry night if I was walking home from that disco in a summer dress), to collective delusion. Journalist Nell McCafferty observed, with her characteristic dry wit, that the way women were treated, no wonder they were taking to the roads. In retrospect, it seems clear that the apparitions were a manifestation of public disquiet concerning the mobility of real-life Irish women. In a decade when news stories reported that women were stepping down off the pedestals on which they had been placed, they could no longer be assumed to be emulating Mary, statically embodying chastity and obedience. As the erstwhile

Children of Mary popped off their plinths, the plaster replica of our moral Mammy was following suit.

Anthropologist Nancy Scheper-Hughes has written on the propensity of Irish society to cause schizophrenia, and you don't have to look any further than the Catholic teaching about Mary, allegedly a mother *and* a Virgin. Aged about nine, I innocently asked the Master what the word virgin meant; he told me it was a woman who hadn't had a child. When I expressed puzzlement about the term being applied to Mary, he told me to go home and ask my mother. Innocent as I was, I rightly suspected that that would have been an unwise move. I kept mum, and kept away from Mam with my awkward questions. Nowadays, I'm still reassessing Mary's role. After all, perhaps a teenager who found herself pregnant by someone who thought they were God is an appropriate role model for Irish women.

The Kerry Babies Case was a watershed. After that, people lost faith in the judiciary being on their side. The Tribunal was supposed to investigate how and why the Hayes family came to confess to a murder they did not commit. Instead, it became an examination and condemnation of a woman who, by her lifestyle, exposed some of the hypocrisies surrounding Irish women's lives. Before Joanne Hayes, Eileen Flynn, and Ann Lovett, we were all assumed to be Children of Mary, virginal and chaste before marriage, willing handmaidens of God and husband afterwards. After the death of Lovett, in particular, Irish women began to share their own stories, most often anonymously, by writing and phoning in to radio shows. From the mid-1980s, more disturbing secrets began to emerge. Books and newspaper articles told stories about priests, nuns and other assumed leaders who had abused their authority. Some had raped and assaulted children, others had had affairs, some had fathered 'illegitimate' children. The stories about cruelty in remand schools, Magdalen Laundries and other church-run institutions became more frequent, in all forms of media, in factual accounts and in fiction. It seems to me that the outburst of high profile scandalous stories began with the Kerry Babies Case. Once the misogyny of the Irish judicial system was exposed the bubble had burst. There was no possibility of maintaining the fantasy of a benign authority, of either church or state. The other unpalatable prejudice that was exposed was that of class; the Hayes family were ordinary small farming stock, with limited income and education. They had little defence against the wiles of experienced lawyers out to protect the legal system and its officers. In many of the abuse cases that subsequently came to light, the children and other victims were economically as well as socially vulnerable.

Nell McCafferty's book, *A Woman to Blame: The Kerry Babies Case*, ran to a second edition in 2010, and the Tribunal is much discussed in feminist accounts of Irish society. However, mainstream media seem to be a bit reticent about resurrecting the story. While in Ireland recently, I watched *Reeling in the Years* on RTE, the national broadcaster. Each weekday following the main evening news, significant footage of a chosen year was shown, with an appropriate soundtrack. Seeing that the 1980s were being featured, I looked out for 1984-85. Moving Statues made an appearance, but the Kerry Babies Case was not mentioned. Perhaps the editors wished to spare Joanne Hayes further embarrassment. But it is important that we don't forget. The Kerry Babies Case was a 1980s version of the Salem Witch-hunt. When the case is mentioned now, people ask: 'But what really happened? What's the real story?' Who knows? I don't know what happened to Joanne Hayes's baby, except that it died and was buried. What I do know is that what happened to the child's mother was a crime against Irish womanhood, a crime against humanity, and a crime against justice.

## Further Reading

Gerard Colleran and Michael O'Regan, *Dark Secrets* (Kerryman, 1985)

Joanne Hayes (with John Barrett), *My Story* (Brandon, 1985)

Tom Inglis, *Truth, Power and Lies: Irish Society and the Case of the Kerry Babies* (University College Dublin Press, 2003)

Nell McCafferty, *A Woman to Blame: The Kerry Babies Case* (Attic, 1985)

Barry O'Halloran, *Lost Innocence: The Inside Story of the Kerry Babies Mystery* (Raytown, 1985)

Tim Ryan and Jurek Kirakowski, *Ballinspittle: Moving Statues and Faith* (Mercier, 1985)

Nancy Scheper-Hughes, *Saints, Scholars and Schizophrenics: Mental Illness in Rural Ireland*, (University of California Press, 1977)

# Junior Crime Reporter
## *Peter Mortimer*

It's a strange thing, our response to crime. There's probably no worse crime than murder, which wipes out a life, full stop, yet our attitudes to it are cosy. We play board games like *Cluedo* where we delight in guessing how people were murdered, we give writers prestigious awards for writing about it, (often named after deadly weapons such as The Silver Dagger Award), whole festivals and conventions are held on the literary interpretations of the subject. Can you imagine for one moment any of the above taking place around the crime of rape? The thought is too shocking to contemplate, yet foul though rape is, usually the victim is at least still alive.

The British, despite the inroads of many modern urban crime novelists still hanker after murders that take place in sleepy leafy villages, preferably round the time of the Summer fête and with the vicar hovering close by. Our attitudes to crime remain ambivalent. The *Daily Mail* is capable of working up a national fury at the prospect of overlenient sentencing, and the 'flogging is too good for them' brigade are always in strong voice. Yet simultaneously films and fiction often portray the criminal as some kind of romantic free spirit kicking against the system. Understandably, of late, bank robbers — a dying breed in the age of computer crime — have been seen in a less harsh light than pre-2008. How prescient was Bertolt Brecht when he said there was no difference between robbing a bank and owning a bank? Watching the bank fat cats lick away at their creamy one million pound bonuses while pensioners die of hypothermia is the kind of outrage only a pachyderm such as Jeremy Clarkson would not find repellent.

My own inglorious time as a junior crime reporter on the *Walthamstow Guardian* took in no murders. I doubt it is remembered by anyone in the East London borough of Waltham Forest. Locally the paper was known simply as *The Guardian,* as the national broadsheet of such name made little inroads into these mean streets. I was a fresh-faced reporter just out of university and as is the wont of weekly newspapers — another dying breed — its journalists were expected to be jacks of all trades. I was on the newspaper for two years and at different times took on different roles. For a short time I was the business correspondent ("Mortimer, comb your hair, put a suit and on and get your bloody pic taken on the end of a phone!" shouted the editor, in an attempt to convince readers that such a photo by-line meant here was a journalist with the full grasp of financial affairs.)

One of the main local employers was LR Industries (formerly London Rubber) which manufactured Durex contraceptives. The nudge-nudge possibilities of any story regarding this organisation were obvious, though several of my smutty puns in the LR pieces I filed were struck out by the sub-editors prior to publication, thus denying the great Waltham Forest public the benefit of my wit.

On one occasion I was summoned into the editor's office and told "Mortimer, you're Aunt Elizabeth for three weeks!" Aunt Elizabeth wrote 'Kiddies Corner' with a series of games, observations and stories for nippers. I don't think I've ever been happier in my life. For a period, I became the football correspondent covering Leytonstone FC, a more humble relation of Leyton Orient. I would stamp my frozen feet on the touchline, attempting to wax lyrical about the 22 bruisers kicking hell out of one another in the clogging mud. Which brings me to my time writing about crime. Let me first boast of my greatest claim to fame. I was despatched to a local pub to investigate rumours that it was a centre for drug dealing. This was 1970.

How thrilling and dangerous it felt to be operating undercover. After hanging round for several drinks and chatting to various people, I made casual enquiries about 'scoring', and before too long was offered a tab of acid (LSD). This ended up as the front page lead the following Friday.

## ACID — AT 25p A TRIP!

ran the headline across five columns, and there was my name on the story. The police moved in, I lost all my street cred with any hip friends, and a few days later in the post I received a slightly threatening correspondence, made up of letters cut from a newspaper, telling me to watch out. I was both shocked and secretly thrilled and carefully pasted it into my scrap book along with the story. I heard nothing more.

Most crime reporting was less dramatic and involved sitting on the hard wooden press box seat in the local magistrates court. There was a maxim in weekly newspapers that you should not show too great an aptitude for shorthand, which was still learned in the t-line version by reporters in those far-off days. To do so was to condemn yourself to a life covering either the local council or local magistrates court, both places where reporting demanded great accuracy, but where tedium was a regular companion.

My spell in these courts rapidly robbed me of any romantic associations with the criminal classes. The accused were not mainly the quick-witted attractive characters of film and novels. Here were dysfunctional, often incoherent people unable to deal with the world around them. Burglars usually lacked imagination and broke into the house up the street from them. I would be tempted to stand up and shout, "For God's sake, if you're going to burgle, go for those posh types in Chingford or Epping!" I never did. There was though one occasion in which my verbal ejaculation in court left me seriously embarrassed.

A full session in the magistrates court brought maybe ten cases, not all of which you would report. Some were simply too dull, others involved people from outside the area and often minor misdemeanours involving juveniles (where names could not be used) were of little interest. It was during the hearing of one such juvenile case that I found myself drifting off into reverie, pleasant thoughts of activities elsewhere while the evidence, which I was not reporting, droned on. Suddenly the chairman of the bench asked "Is *The Guardian* in court?"

I shot out of my seat with my arm in the air.

"Yes, sir, here, sir, yes sir!" I responded, with an excess of zeal. Did I hold up notebook and pen as verifying my credentials? I probably did. The magistrate, a pillar of the local establishment as I recall, fixed me with a beady eye, and in somewhat cold terms, with just a hint of contempt said,"I am talking, you fool, about the guardian of the child."

I slunk back into my seat, as every eye in the court swivelled to take in this buffoon.

Such things never happened to Aunt Elizabeth.

# Dando the Oyster-Eater: The Life and Times of a Bouncing, Seedy Swell on a Bilking Spree
## *Ann Featherstone*

*"I refuse to starve in a land of plenty. Instead I shall follow the example of my betters by running into debt without having the means of paying. Why, some men live in great extravagance and luxury, owe money and cheat their creditors, yet they are still considered respectable and honest. I only run into debt to satisfy the craving of hunger, and yet I am despised and beaten."*

**Edward Dando**, April 1832

When he was discharged from a London police court in April 1832 where he had been summoned on a charging of bilking, Dando was not intent on making political mileage when he offered his personal philosophy to a crowd of onlookers outside.[1] In fact, he was more eager to find the next bilking opportunity and satisfy his ever-present hunger. But the economic environment of Britain in the 1830s made his views on surviving in a land of plenty *for the few*, nevertheless, pertinent. Corrupt banking practices and government bail-outs were rife, massive personal and national debt were crippling, along with rising unemployment and desperate poverty. There was civil unrest: the Swing Riots amongst agricultural workers in south-east spread north, reaching the Midlands and over the water in France, revolution shook class complacency. All of which was an ironic backdrop to Dando's particular criminal exploits.

April 1832 was by no means his first court appearance. Two years earlier, Mr Mason, oyster-stall keeper, had him arrested for eating eleven dozen (132) oysters, a half-quartern loaf and eleven pats of butter without having the money to pay for them.[2] "If I have not got money, where is the use of detaining me. As the saying goes, you can't draw blood from a stone." The oysterman was unconvinced by his argument at which Dando tried to make a run for it, and would have got away had not a policeman made an opportune appearance and stopped him. Mr Mason, a very reasonable fellow under the circumstances, declared in court that if Dando had just eaten a few dozen of his oysters he would have let him go, "but it was the fact," he told the magistrate, "that he punished such a quantity." Dando remained charmingly unapologetic: if he was hungry, he said, he must eat and that was that. Mr Swabey, one of the court officials, said that Mr Mason would have been perfectly justified in taking the coat off Dando's back in recompense, but the oysterman declared that there was little point: if he sold all the bilker's clothes it would not raise a shilling. Instead, he expressed the desire to give Dando "a good sound thrashing with this cane I hold in my hand which would in some measure compensate me for the loss of my bread and oysters." This he did, lying in wait for Dando, when he discharged from the court.

The case was widely reported in many local newspapers as well as the London dailies. All were characterised by a tone which was half-amused, half amazed. By the time he died in 1833, Dando had established a considerable reputation for his bilking crimes and prodigious appetite, his name falling into colloquialism.[3] His exploits were told (and embellished) in verse, articles and in a popular farce, *Dandolo; or the Last of the Doges,* for the City of London Theatre in 1838 based on William Thackeray's short story, *The Professor*. The excesses of Dando had a strange appeal. In an age where those able to afford to *pay* for one of Dando's famous blow-outs were the very privileged few, his audacity drew a sneaking admiration from the more cynical newspaper men and perhaps, even the hard-pressed working poor. Though he undoubtedly broke the law and spent much time in prison — in Brixton he had to be kept in solitary confinement because he robbed other prisoners of their allowance of bread and beef — there was an eccentric charm about his unscrupulousness and bravado as well as an awful fascination with the vast quantities he enjoyed eating.

Dando liked all food in quantity, but his favourites were oysters, the fast-food of the early 19th century. Oyster-stalls, like those of Mr Mason, could be found on many street-corners where 'natives' were expertly shucked and delivered with vinegar, slices of bread and pats of butter extra. They were cheap and plentiful. As Sam Weller remarks,

> It's a wery remarkable circumstance, sir, that poverty and oysters always seems to go together ... the poorer a place is the great call there seems to be for oysters ... Blessed if I don't think that ven a man's wery poor he rushes out of his lodgings and eats oysters in reg'lar desperation.

Shops as well as stalls sold oysters. One of Dando's greatest feats was to order and eat thirteen dozen (156) oysters with five bottles of ginger beer at Mrs Hamell's oyster shop. The ginger beer, Dando said, was medicinal as he was "troubled with wind in the stomach." Hardly surprising, perhaps, but it was commonly believed that the oyster was an eminently digestible food, never causing indigestion. "You may eat them today, tomorrow, for ever and as many of them as you are able," claimed a write in *All the Year Round*. "The Oyster's presence in the stomach is hardly perceptible." But given that the weight of a dozen oysters, "including water", was estimated at four ounces (113gm), Dando's punishment of thirteen dozen at Mrs Hamell's establishment meant that, without ginger beer, he ate over three pounds (1.3kg) in weight. He ate them uncooked and probably unadorned, and this seems to have been the preferred method of the purist. "Let me stand at a fair counter with its pure marble top," wrote 'Our Own Dando' in Tom Hood's satirical magazine, *Fun*, "and there calmly and with fine appreciation take an exquisite mouthful from its pearly shell in the moment after it hath been revealed by the knife of the honest man who opens it."

Oysters were readily and easily available, but although the 1830s was a decade of want, food shops and stalls, coffee houses and taverns crowded the London streets and filled the air with tempting aromas and generous servings. Dando blamed the "savory smell of sundry rounds of beef" in the open window of a cook-shop for enticing him in for a blow-out. Anderson's à la Mode Beef House on Drury Lane was one of the very popular eating-houses that served up the nineteenth-century equivalent of a rich beef stew and, like oysters, another fast-food. Here, he ordered a large plate of à-la-mode, a salad well-dressed and a pint of ale.[4] He called for a second plate with salad and a glass of brandy. When he called for a third helping, the landlord became anxious and requested payment for what had already been eaten — with the usual result.

In his courtroom performances, Dando provided good newspaper copy: he had a sharp wit and an easy manner and provided reporters with striking quotes. "A man cannot starve in a free country," he observed. When Sir Richard Birnie, the police magistrate, pointed out that a man could not eat and drink at the expense of others, Dando retorted, "Why, Sir Richard, I am not exactly singular in that respect." He considered himself no thief and hard done to to be imprisoned for incurring a debt without the means of paying whilst his 'betters' did the same thing with impunity. The irony was, of course, that the people Dando failed to pay in his bilking sprees were often the very people who could least afford it — the street oyster-seller, the coffee-shop keeper and fishmonger

— all of whom had to be on the look-out for him. Indeed, by the end of his short career, Dando's reputation made him more recognisable than at its commencement when he was simply described as 'shabby-genteel.' The *Morning Chronicle* felt it a duty to alert 'oyster-dealers and the public in general' when he was released from gaol, along with an up-to-date physical description:

> He stands about five feet seven inches in height — 29 years of age, and is lame of the right foot. His hair is brown — complexion fair — and he generally wears a gaol dress.

Dando's dress eventually became a problem. With a shabby-genteel appearance, he must have given the impression of being able to pay for his food. But as his periods of imprisonment increased and he looked more and more shabby (and less genteel), that impression was more difficult to sustain. In 1830, he was forced to 'sneak' into Rouse's fish-shop whilst Miss Rouse's back was turned and had ordered and eaten two dozen of her best oysters before she spotted him and wondered if his tastes were not 'too extravagant for a poor man.' Six months and a couple of periods of gaol-time later, he crept into a 'snug corner' of Anderson's Beef House but still pulled off the 'sell' by ordering 'in the tone of a man with a thousand a year.' By 1831, Dando cut a very bizarre figure being dressed entirely in institutional clothes — jacket, waistcoat and trousers from Brixton and Guildford Prisons and Middlesex House of Correction, and his shirt, stockings and shoes courtesy of the City Authorities.

There were, of course, Dando imitators during his lifetime, including a 'cadaverous-looking wight' by the name of Flunder, who consumed a double plate of roast pork, vegetables and bread, followed by three platefuls of hot boiled leg of mutton with vegetables and bread and was declared he didn't have the 4s/3d he owed, but would pay it when he could. *Female* Dandos appeared. A 'thin, pale-looking girl' who ate five dozen oysters with bread, butter and porter and, having not a 'scurrick' with which to pay for them, offered to leave her bonnet which, of course, was not worth sixpence. One of the most engaging was the well-built, six foot three inch *gourmandisere* who tried to bilk her way out of the Castle Tavern, owned by the champion pugilist, Tom Spring. When she was tackled by Bishop, the waiter, and Tom Spring in person, she declared that her bill would be settled by her 'particular friends' and Spring, bowing to his 'natural gallantry to the fair sex', did not pursue the matter. (It is hinted by the writer of the article that the 'lady' might have been a life guardsman!)[5]

Dando died in September 1832, aged (perhaps) thirty. The *Morning Post* reported that he had recently arrived in London from Kent (where he had been imprisoned several times on bilking charges), had been arrested only days before and sent to Coldbath Fields Prison. There he fell victim to cholera which that year struck London with devastating effect, killing over 6,000 people in twelve months. The *Morning Post* gave a strangely detailed account of Dando's last hours:

> On Tuesday afternoon, about five o'clock, he was violently attacked with cholera, and could not move off the seat he was sitting on. A beggar, named Martin, went to assist him, and he was removed to the infirmary. In a very short time after Martin was also attacked with cholera, and they both died in a few hours afterwards, within an hour of each other, and were buried on Wednesday afternoon.[6]

There followed a small rash of elegies, odes and dirges in newspapers and journals, all comic and many tongue-in-cheek. The *Elegy on the Death of Dando, the Ostracide*[7] gave the writer licence to pun outrageously on the names of poets,

> *Lamb* he [Dando] devour'd, and his delight was *Shelley,*
> Gloated on *Crabbe,* and sometimes *Sprat* embraced –

philosophers, seafood and place names,

> To banquet on six bushels, for a meal
> At Hythe of *Dover,* — where he ate a *Deal*!

Barnard Gregory's notorious weekly, *The Satirist; or, the Censor of the Times* offered a memorial inscription to the 'immortal Dando' including the suggestion that, ironically, it was the oyster itself which carried the cholera that killed the ostreophagist:

> The fatal cholera, sweeping on our shores,
> Could not so quickly carry off its scores;
> So, envious of his huge devouring fame,
> To blight his glories like a demon came.
> Knowing the object of his constant wish,
> It slyly lurked within the tempting fish.
> Now, he, alas! and who our grief can tell
> Lies, like his darling oyster, in his *shell*.[8]

It was *The Life and Death of Dando, the Celebrated Oyster Glutton*, published by Catnach, the ballad-monger of Seven Dials and so, perhaps, sold as a broadsheet, which located Dando in the tradition of mythical figures. In this 'catch' he became a grotesque, with a gigantic mouth — a *'flounder mouth* for *mutton pies'* — and a ragged appearance — 'His coat was rusty, hole-y and fat,/His hair was like an old door-mat.' A man on his uppers — 'His Sunday dress went *up the spout'*, that is in pawn — Dando's crimes were, ironically, those of the swaggering 'bouncers' in the banks, financial houses and even aristocracy and government who swindled, cheated and lied. The eloquent Dando of the police courts with his proto-political protest, the scourge of the eating-house and oyster-stall became a 'bouncing, seedy swell'.

> Dando, he's gone to *feed the worms,*
> With him they'll live on very good terms.
> So *Dando oysters* the folks can sell –
> Dando, the bouncing, seedy swell.

[1] Bilk, v.: to deceive, cheat; defraud, fail to pay; elude, evade. Bilker, n: a cheater, swindler. All these colloquialisms arose in Restoration days and all had become Standard English by 1850. (Partridge, *The Penguin Dictionary of Historical Slang*, 1972.)

[2] Half-quartern loaf: a quarter loaf was made with three and a half pounds of flour, the finished loaf weighing in at around four and a quarter pounds. A half-quartern loaf was still substantial at just over two pounds in weight. Pats of butter: these are likely to be larger than today's small, individually wrapped morsels.

[3] Dando: a heavy eater; especially one who cheats restaurants, cafes, hotels.

[4] *Mrs Beeton's recipe for Beef à la mode* (1861). Ingredients – about 3lbs of clod or flank of beef, 2oz of clarified dripping, 1 large onion, flour, a quart of water, 12 berries of allspice, 2 bay-leaves, ½ teaspoon of whole black pepper, salt to taste. Mode – cut the beef into small pieces, and roll them in flour; put the dripping into a stew-pan with the onion, which should be sliced thin. Let it get quite hot; lay in the pieces of beef, and stir them well about. When nicely browned all over, add *by degrees* boiling water in the above proportion, and, as the water is added, keep the whole well stirred. Put in the spice, bay-leaves, and seasoning, cover the stewpan closely, and set it by the side of the fire to stew *very gently*, till the meat becomes quite tender, which will be in about 3 hours, when it will be ready to serve.

Other recipes include the addition of wine or brandy. It was generally served with a salad, 'well-dressed' meaning exactly as it does today – a dressing of oil and vinegar.

[5] The report is found in *Bell's Life in London and Sporting Chronicle* (5 August 1832), the leading sporting newspaper of the time, and a fine resource for topics of social interest.

[6] *Morning Post,* 1 September 1832.

[7] 'Elegy on the Death of Dando, the Ostracide', *Tait's Edinburgh Magazine*, January, 1833.

[8] 'The Death of Dando', *The Satirist; or the Censor of the Times*, 2 September, 1832.

# "I Loved Charlie"
## The Amazing Criminal Exploits and Astounding Cultural Afterlife of the Great Portico Thief Charles Peace
### *Michael Eaton*

When I was little child my grandma would sing:

> I used to be Napoleon in the waxworks show
> All the people they admired me so
> But now I've had bad luck
> They've melted down my grease
> They've put me in the Chamber of Horrors
> And called me Charlie Peace.

Tales of this night prowler scared me, though in time I came to believe he was a fairy-tale bogey man, a made-up creature of folklore. Only when I saw his terrifying effigy in the Chamber of Horrors did I realise Charles Peace had been all too real. Nana told me that he lived in Nottingham, down in Narrow Marsh. But there was no mention of that in any account I read, so I supposed she had made it up — we have a long-standing habit of embracing criminal folk-heroes round here. But if Charles Peace had simply been the most successful cat burglar of his day and age, is it likely that his name would be used to frighten children almost a century later? Was it Peace the girls were chanting about when the skipping-rope twirled in the playground?

> I loved Charlie, Charlie was a thief
> Charlie killed a copper, Charlie came to grief
> Charlie came to your house, stole a leg of beef
> Charlie came to our house, stole some bread and jam
> Ate me mother's pudding, ate me father's ham

When the coppers caught him hung him on a rope
Poor old Charlie... hasn't got a hope.

Why did this robber and double-murderer become in popular consciousness a legendary trickster, a Robin Hood of the public prints? Why was he turned into a folk-hero even before his execution? Why was he memorialised, at first in Penny Dreadfuls, waxwork shows and travelling fairground theatres, then later in films and comic strips?

The man they called 'The King Of The Lags' was born in Sheffield in the early 1830s. His father worked on a travelling show with trained, caged lions and tigers before he settled down and became a zealous convert to evangelical Christianity. If Charlie had inherited his dad's show-business career would he have turned to the bad? When his childhood was over he was apprenticed in the hell of a South Yorkshire steel mill. Charlie had an unexpected fourteenth birthday present when a length of white hot metal shot through his leg. His very survival was amazing, the saving of his limb little short of miraculous. He not only learned to walk again but became a contortionist of immense agility. This accident was the turning-point. He made a pledge to himself that henceforth no man would ever be his mester. He would never do an honest day's work again. Peace declared war upon respectable society.

He was a fine musician, playing, appropriately, the fiddle, billed in low music halls as 'The Modern Paganini'. But his musicianship acted as a cover for a much more profitable trade: house-breaking and cat burglary, and his violin case hid the tools of that trade. Peace was a master of disguise and a ferocious fighter. He had no fear of anyone, eluding a disorganised police force for many years until his inevitable capture.

Charlie Peace was in and out of gaol for the next eighteen years under various aliases and prison regimes, imprisoned under the silent system at Millbank, flogged for organising a prison mutiny in Dartmoor. Finally released in 1872, now aged about forty, he determined never to see the inside of a prison again. His wife, Hannah, had remained loyal to him whilst he was banged up and now they outwardly maintained a respectable existence in the patriotically named Victoria Terrace on Britannia Road in Darnall near Sheffield — a fine location for a man who gave 'darn all'.

And then he met the beautiful Missis Dyson. Peace had always exerted a charismatic charm over the opposite sex and Katherine Dyson was far from immune to his blandishments. She was an Irish-American woman who moved in next-door-but-one with her husband, Arthur, who had been a railroad engineer in the States. Though later, somewhat unconvincingly, she publicly denied intimacy, their torrid affair must have been conducted right under the noses of their respective spouses. In time, however, the magnetic attraction Katherine once felt for this villainous neighbour turned into terror. Peace did not take easily to being spurned. His lust mutated into obsession. Like a man possessed, his twisted passion began to affect the delicate balance of his work.

On a job in Manchester he slipped up and was about to be caught, when he took out his pistol and shot a policeman. Now he had crossed the line. He was a cop killer. His luck held out though. The police pinned the shooting on an innocent Irish labourer: a case of 'Round up the usual Fenians!' But this was not an act of political terrorism but Ordinary Decent Criminality.

Peace brazenly attended the trial of young William Habron for the murder of Police Constable Cock. He was even heard complaining that the evidence against the young Irish lad was merely circumstantial as he sat, in disguise as a clergyman, in the public gallery. Habron was found guilty and sentenced to death despite his desperate pleas of innocence. Fortunately the jury recommended mercy because of his youth and the verdict was commuted to imprisonment for life.

The Dysons moved out of the area, but if Arthur thought he could evade his wife's tormentor he was sorely mistaken. Peace tracked them down to Banner Cross on the posh side of town, the western edge not far from the Peaks, where they lived in a house still standing today.

One November night Charlie appeared like a wraith, collaring Katherine as she stepped out to the privy and finally blowing away poor Mister Dyson in his own back yard as his wife looked on in horror.

Peace was on the run with a considerable reward of one hundred pounds on his head. That was when he came to Nottingham — I should never have doubted my Nana. He holed up in a cheap gaff in the crime-ridden no-go zone of the Marsh, shamelessly continuing to pursue his chosen profession. And there he fell in love again.

Susan Gray was one of her names, another was Sue Bailey. She shared a love of music with the man she came to know as 'Jack Thompson'. Saturday night was the Music Hall; Sunday morning was the Chapel. Her beautiful voice was a great attraction to this supposed travelling salesman. When they set up as man and wife neither of them thought it significant to tell the other they were both already married. Did Sue know what Jack was up to when he went out to work whilst the city slept? She soon found out when the knock on the door came early one morning. She opened up to find two policemen standing there. Her 'husband' leapt out of an upstairs window and legged it into the lawless warrens.

Later a message came for her to join him in London where a brass plaque outside his Peckham house proclaimed him: 'Dealer In And Repairer Of Musical Instruments'. They unusually shared their genteel South London home with another woman. 'Jack' told the uncomplaining Sue this was his 'mother', Missis Ward — actually she was none other than long-suffering Hannah Peace. Sweet Sue was unknowingly sharing a *ménage à trois*!

Inhabitants of the suburbs of South London found themselves victims of a one-man crime wave. The Thompsons were popular neighbours, holding soirées presided over by the Master of the House on his violin accompanying Sue's lovely singing voice. Sometimes he would make his excuses to be called out on an important matter of business only to return home later when his guests were somewhat worse for wear from the generous gin-soaked hospitality doled out by the old lady. Coincidentally, some guests would return home to find their homes had been burgled.

One day Sue must have accidentally discovered that not only that 'the mother' was really 'the wife' but that the man in her life was, in fact, the notorious Banner Cross Murderer! From that day forth Hannah kept her under virtual house arrest, plying her with spirits and snuff to keep her quiet and befuddled.

On an autumn night in 1878, Peace was caught in the act by Constable Edward Robinson whilst robbing a villa in Blackheath. Charlie's revolver flashed and the policeman was wounded, shot in the arm. The heroic Blue Lobster managed to keep hold of his murderous assailant. Upon arrest the burglar gave his name as 'John Ward' but otherwise kept silent.

A pretty young woman, it would seem, turned up at the Greenwich police station, claiming the hundred pound reward for the Sheffield killer. Only then did the police realise that the man sitting calmly reading the Bible in their holding cell, the man they thought was a 'mulatto' as his face was dyed with walnut juice, might be the infamous Charles Peace, The Banner Close Murderer.

Peace made a daring escape from the train taking him back up north for his hearing. But he was caught once again and finally convicted after a trial at the Crown Court in Leeds which galvanised Victorian society. For Katherine Dyson was brought back from the States to testify against him, branding the prisoner in the dock 'a devil', denying she had ever had an affair with him. The jury returned a verdict within minutes: Guilty!

Charlie was an untroubled prisoner who, in the death cell, made a model of a cardboard Gothic monument which he wished to be his tomb, rather resembling the Albert Memorial. But before his last day on this earth he made an astounding confession. It was he who had shot the young policeman in Whalley Range, Manchester. The coppers had committed perjury to convict that young Irish lad.

William Habron was released from hard labour as Peace walked to the gallows.

Before the drop Charlie refused the hood to cover his eyes and addressed the assembled gentlemen of the press: 'You know what my life has been. Tell all my friends I feel sure that I am going into the Kingdom of Heaven. Goodbye and Amen!'

\*\*\*

That was not the end of the story. Charlie Peace's life and crimes instantly struck a chord amongst the labouring populace; they certainly kept his memory green.

Though the days of the broadside ballad, the 'Chorus From The Gallows' sold at the foot of the scaffold, were long over, Charlie's exploits were still memorialised in poetry and song. Within hours of The Banner Cross Murder an enterprising letter-press printer, William Rose of Steelhouse Lane, Sheffield, got busy putting out the first ballad versifying the murder of Arthur Dyson. And Charlie continued to crop in popular Music Hall numbers such as 'I'm 'Enery the Eighth, I am.'

Once 'John Ward' was unmasked as Charles Peace the press covered his exploits in great detail. But none of the more respectable prints came close to rivalling the coverage given by *The Illustrated Police News*. This weekly with its garish cover page, published by George Purkess of The Strand, was called 'The Worst Newspaper In England' by a Grub Street rival jealous of its massive circulation of 200,000 copies per week. Charlie made the cover nine issues on the trot with graphic illustrations depicting iconic incidents: The Murder Of Dyson, The Shooting Of Robinson, The Escape From The Train, The Walk To The Scaffold. No other criminal came close until an unknown serial murderer stalked the streets of Whitechapel.

Even before the execution Purkess was advertising another forthcoming publication: *Charles Peace — Or The Adventures Of A Notorious Burglar*. Retailing at one penny per week this Penny Dreadful was eagerly devoured by the newly literate multitude, running for one hundred issues totalling eight hundred pages, and reissued under hard covers in several editions well into the twentieth century. Each issue had an action-packed woodcut on the title page. Presented gratis in Part One was a lurid full colour folio-sized print of *Charles Peace's Dream On the Night Of His Execution*. This is a most extraordinary publication. For the first few numbers evidently little was yet known of the truth of the eponymous burglar, so an entirely fictional story was concocted to pad it out. As the run continued, however, more and more primary sources were plagiarised verbatim, making this volume an extraordinary research resource.

It's hardly surprisingly that Charlie often makes an appearance whenever a story or song is set in a Waxworks Museum, for Madame Tussaud's instantly snapped up Peace-iana and displayed no less than two wax effigies of him. One showed a creepy, menacing figure whilst the other depicted a contrite Charlie in the presence of William Marwood the Hangman, inventor of the long drop method of 'humane execution'. These were exhibited in The Chamber of Horrors well into the 1960s. Scotland Yard's Black Museum also preserves some priceless items of memorabilia including his violin, his burglary tools and the fold-away ladder he used for scaling. Sheffield's Police Museum can hardly compete, with only a pair of his glasses proudly on display, but it does contain an effigy of the native son in one of the cells.

Charlie Peace is one of the few 'true life' criminals to be named in a Sherlock Holmes story. In *The Illustrious Client* (1927) Conan Doyle has his consulting detective remark:

> 'A complex mind. All great criminals have that. My old friend Charlie Peace was a violin virtuoso.'

Though how Holmes could ever have known him when Peace was living incognito in London is never explained.

Charlie had previously made an appearance in *Gentlemen and Players* (1899) by Conan Doyle's brother-in-law E. W. Hornung. His Old Etonian cracksman A.J. Raffles makes the case:

> 'To follow Crime with reasonable impunity you simply must have a parallel, ostensible career — the more public the better... Mister Peace, of pious memory, disarmed suspicion by acquiring a local reputation for playing the fiddle and taming animals. Fill the bill in some prominent part and you'll never be suspected of doubling it with another of equal prominence... That's the one and only reason why I don't burn my cricket bats for firewood.'

Mark Twain uses Charlie to have a dig at the public fascination with celebrity criminals in the last story he published, his satirical squib *Captain Stormfield's Visit to Heaven* (1909):

> '(T)he finest thing that has happened (up in Heaven) in my day... was Charles Peace's reception — him they called 'the Bannercross Murderer', an Englishman. There were four patriarchs and two prophets on the Grand Stand that time. There hasn't been anything like it since Captain Kidd came...'

Mrs Belloc Lowndes' shocker of the London fog *The Lodger* (1913) might have been inspired by the exploits of Jack the Ripper, but this didn't stop Charlie from ingratiating himself into the tale. The heroine, Daisy Bunting, and her father are given a tour of the Black Museum:

> 'In this here little case are the tools of Charles Peace... Many gents as comes here thinks this case the most

interesting of all. Peace was such a wonderful man! A great inventor they say he would have been, had he been put in the way of it. Here's his ladder; you see it folds up quite compactly, and makes a nice little bundle — just like a bundle of old sticks any man might have been seen carrying about London... without attracting any attention. Why, it probably helped him to look like an honest working man time and time again... My word, he was artful!'

Even the prolific Edgar Wallace got in on the act, casting Peace as *The Devil Man* (1931). Dictated in the course of a weekend, it takes longer to read than it took the author to write! Here Charlie has few redeeming features, the publisher's blurb thundering: 'He was a repulsive creature to look upon; a colossal braggart; a gifted musician; a murderer; a dwarf in stature and a Samson in strength; the perfect burglar...', not forgetting to stress that Peace was 'a man with an irresistible attraction for women.'

Bills from the travelling theatres advertised plays which continued to be performed long after his death. The text of one of these 'Plays For The People' is still extant, that of Joe Hodson of Swallownest, Yorks. In this piece Charlie has become a truly popular rebel, a silver-tongued lover secretly dispersing the profits of his crimes among the poor and dispossessed, including a Dickensian crossing-sweeper. The hero, it goes without saying, mounts the scaffold with a swagger and without regret.

So it comes as no surprise that Charlie's story was embraced by a new medium of narrative sensation. Two cinematograph productions were released in 1905, possibly the first 'factual dramas' to be made in this land. The wonderful *Life of Charles Peace* by William Haggar, a travelling showman in South Wales, survives as an early masterpiece of the British cinema. Haggar's son, Walter, plays Charlie as a villain of melodrama. His outrageous exploits must have been taken to their bosoms by the working-class audiences in the mining

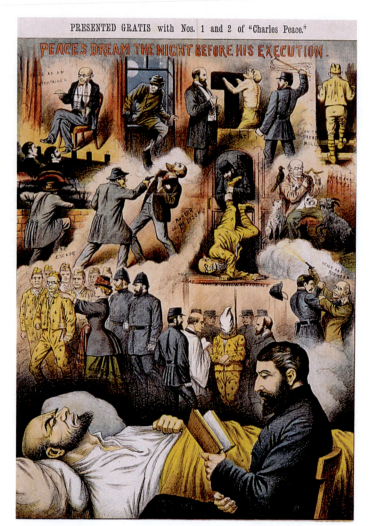

Photo courtesy of the National Fairground Archive, University of Sheffield Library

communities of the valleys. He's always on the move, a shape-shifter incarnate. The relish with which he metes out violence towards a variety of comic policemen is especially prominent, causing magistrates and clergymen to denounce the film's potential influence upon the minds of the young and ignorant. The final scene of Peace's execution was considered particularly shocking.

The other film from the same year came from the Mottershaw film company based in Peace's own home town and now unfortunately lost. Their advertisement explicitly states that this more tasteful enterprise certainly does not, unlike its competitor, depict the hanging. But the shot-by-shot description that does remain proclaims an unrivalled realism, for the scenes depicting the murder of Dyson and Peace's attempt to escape from the train were shot in the actual locations at Banner Cross and Shireoaks.

The only sound film was a low-budget but nevertheless interesting Monarch production made in 1949. *The Case of Charles Peace*, directed by Norman Lee and starring Michael Martin Harvey, concentrates on the William Habron miscarriage of justice story and the trial of Peace.

But it was in a comic that kids of my generation were introduced to the 'Arch Rogue of Victorian London'. *The Astounding Adventures of Charlie Peace* ran as a strip in *Buster* from the mid-1960s to the early 1980s. In these beautifully drawn, subtly subversive stories for the nation's children any mention of amorous dalliances has been expunged from the record and Charlie is transformed into a loveable rogue whose antagonists were not so much the 'Crushers' (police) as Scrooge-like exploitative capitalists and criminals far more hard-hearted than himself. There was even a series of stories in which he was 'tricked into entering a time machine' and found himself in a modern Britain of Mini cars and mini-skirts — a world which, needless to say, he found more confusing than his own Victorian past.

The mass media transformed a Life into a Legend, a Man into a Myth. Why was this common criminal the focus of such multitudinous makeovers? Could it be that Peace's life and crimes offered a resounding 'No' to his society's sanctimonious illusion that honest toil leads to material prosperity? He cocked a shameless snook at notions of the sanctity of private property and domestic, matrimonial bliss. Accepting no authority but his own, he lived out the unspoken desires of the down-trodden. Charlie Peace was the ambiguous focus of troubling fascination, the Rampant Id, the Trickster, the Dionysiac Bringer of Chaos.

# The Dark Eyes of London
## *Cathi Unsworth*

> I wander thro' each charter'd street,
> Near where the charter'd Thames does flow,
> And mark in every face I meet
> Marks of weakness, marks of woe.

Although it was written over 200 years ago, William Blake's *London* still seems to surmise the motivations of the writers I want to talk about today. Since their nineteenth century beginnings, there have been two distinct types of crime fiction abroad in our capital. There are those, like the original Penny Dreadfuls, that make mass-market entertainment out of murder and its associated horrors.

Then there are those for whom the city is an integral force in a larger picture of crime, corruption and its effects on society. Those who, like Blake, observe their times from the bottom up with the realisation that the biggest criminals who walk amongst us are usually those put in charge of us. It is this mix of the great and the good with the down and the dirty, living and mixing in closer proximity here than perhaps any other city on earth, that fascinates them.

The writers I'm going to talk about today have all used their work to ask serious questions about our ever-shifting populous and to probe the psyche of the times. They share a broadly leftwards leaning, an affinity with the damaged and neglected, an urge to take those responsible for public policy to task, and a need to try and understand how the past impacts on the present. Perhaps more crucially, none of them felt comfortable in the worlds they were born into or took the paths they were supposed to have followed. Maybe only an outsider can ever look in with such clarity.

During the course of my own writing about London, I have gained the impression that time works in a loop here. There are always echoes of previous generations in the work of my chosen writers, as if authors instinctively pick up the threads their predecessors left for them to find. Which is why this talk has a habit of ping-ponging backwards even as it moves forwards.

My story doesn't begin in the present, but in the time that irrevocably shaped the way we live now, and with a writer whose reaction to all that would change the course of crime fiction and what it could be used for. In the fateful year of 1984, Derek Raymond's *He Died With His Eyes Open* was a devastating realisation of Margaret Thatcher's curse: 'There's no such thing as society', from its first line on:

> He was found in the shrubbery in front of the Word of God House in Albatross Road, West Five. It was the thirtieth of March, during the evening rush-hour. It was bloody cold and an office worker had tripped over the body when he was caught short going home. I don't know if you know Albatross Road where it runs into Hangar Lane, but if you do you'll appreciate what a ghastly lonely area it is, with the surface-level tube station on one side of the street, and dank, blind buildings, weeping with damp, on the other.

At once, it's a realistic description of an unlovely part of London usually rushed past by commuters on the A4 and an Existentialist vision of what has caused its decline. A body dumped outside a charismatic church that both God and his flock have long since deserted, on a thoroughfare that doesn't actually exist but alludes instead to Coleridge's *Rime of the Ancient Mariner* for reasons that will shortly become clear.

The journey to Albatross Road is a story of crime and atonement few authors can rival, being as Derek Raymond is the only one of them to have spent the early Sixties working for associates of Reg and Ronnie Kray after having been sent down from the same institution that gave us David Cameron. The erstwhile Robert William Arthur Cook, born in Baker Street in 1931, saw both sides of the class and criminal divide during his remarkable lifetime. 'An Eton background,' he always said, 'is a terrific help if you are into vice of any kind.'

His first novel, 1962's *The Crust on its Uppers* described exactly the kind of capers the youthful Cook got up to in post-War, pre-Swinging London — international art smuggling, running long firms and bent casinos out of King's Road spielers. The book was laced with so much criminal parlance it provided its own glossary, which Eric Partridge, compiler of *The Dictionary of Slang*, said was his best new source in twenty-five years. From the city that invented the term, the use of shortened language and the codes of the street are essential components of all the books I'll talk about today.

In lacing his prose with argot, Cook was following a tradition of Thirties and Forties writers he admired — the American hardboiled greats, Jim Thompson, Raymond Chandler and David Goodis, and their lesser-known, British contemporaries Gerald Kersh, Patrick Hamilton, James Curtis and Alexander Baron, whose underworld landscapes of tatty bedsits and shabby nightclubs, haunted by conmen, Fascists and tarts, share a vivid connection with his own.

But those names were long forgotten in 1984, and *He Died With His Eyes Open* appeared like a lone voice shouting against the crowd. Cook had been absent for London for decades. He'd spent most of the Seventies in Italy, writing vicious satires like *Private Parts, Public Places* and the nightmare dystopia *A State of Denmark* while acting as Foreign Minister for his local anarchist collective. There was a brief, grim sojourn spent back in the Capital, behind the wheel of a mini-cab, before he retreated to France and the life of a labourer. Then a neighbour goaded him that he'd never write a book again.

His response was an act symbolic with death and rebirth. The narrator of the passage I just read is an unnamed Detective Sergeant working a grim adjunct of the Met called A14, Unexplained Deaths: 'by far the most unpopular and shunned branch of the service,' as he goes on to explain: 'We work on obscure, unimportant, irrelevant deaths of people who don't matter and never did.' The DS is a fortysomething with no ambitions for promotion, a failed husband and father haunted by the spectres of his institutionalised wife Edie, and their daughter Dahlia, whom Edie pushed under a bus 'on the afternoon of Hitler's birthday, April 20th, 1979.'

'Where I go, the ghosts go,' the DS considers. His only solace comes from working the beat no one else wants, avenging the unquiet, uncared for dead.

The man The DS hovers over at the opening of *He Died With His Eyes Open* was once Charles Staniland, 51, wearing a cheap suit and a boozer's nose. He has been systematically beaten to death. The DS discovers Staniland's past through a series of cassette tapes left in his bedsit in Romilly Pace, Lewisham.

Staniland had variously worked as a mini-cab driver, a labourer on a French vineyard, and a writer with a strong sense of social conscience. It is the old Robin Cook who lies broken on Albatross Road. The newly rechristened Derek Raymond, his purpose finally realised, stands in the rain beside him.

Raymond's new personae continued to work his lonely and often terrifying beat for five more novels, *The Devil's Home on Leave*, *How the Dead Live*, *I Was Dora Suarez* and *Dead Man Upright,* until the author's death in 1993. His DS stalks the badlands of an ungentrified city — grim housing estates in the Elephant, dreary terraces in Catford, the crumbling remains of Rotherhithe Docks, villain's pubs with darkly humorous monikers — the Nine Foot Drop in Hammersmith, The Henry of Agincourt in Battersea — sex clubs in Soho where atrocities against women are served up as entertainment; all circling back to his base in West 1, whose moniker would bestow this series of novels with a name:

> It's called the Factory by the villains because it has a bad reputation for doing subjects over in the interrogation rooms; people who still think our British policemen are wonderful ought to spend a night or three at the Factory banged up or put under the light by a team of three. We call it the Factory too, but, if you want to know, it's the big, modern, concrete police station... in Poland Street, bang opposite Marks & Sparks.

Informed by Raymond's past life, these London streets form geographical flashpoints to which our next authors will all return. Already his life was intertwined with the next of them. In the months before he died, Raymond was looked after by John Williams, the Cardiff-born writer who is now his literary executor, responsible for the reissues of the Factory series on Serpent's Tail. Williams has probably had the most active role of anyone creating contemporary voices in crime fiction, both in his role as an editor for the aforementioned imprint, and through the impact of his own work.

A former punk rocker, Williams followed his musical muse up to London in the late Seventies, where he worked as a journalist and in a succession of book and record shops. While he was devouring the stock of one such establishment, the much-missed Compendium bookstore in Camden, he had an idea for a book about an emerging new wave of American writers whose work would prove as instrumental as Derek Raymond's in shaping the new voices of British crime fiction.

In his resulting travelogue, 1991's *Into The Badlands* Williams focussed on authors who had big things to say about history and society and whose work was infused with an intoxicating sense of place. These included a trinity of James — Crumley, Lee Burke and Ellroy. It was the latter, whose masterwork LA Quartet began with the story of a doomed girl dubbed *The Black Dahlia* and wove an intricate secret history of his home city in the Forties and Fifties, based on the real crimes and political shenanigans of those times, who would have the most major impact on our writers to come.

Williams had his own things to say about violated women and miscarriages of justice when he returned to the recent past to write 1995's *Bloody Valentine*, an investigation into the murder of 19-year-old Lynette White in Cardiff docks on Valentine's Day 1988. What Williams had intended to be a journalistic account of the crime and subsequent framing of five black men, three of whom served two years before having their convictions quashed, was suppressed itself by a libel action from the police and had to be rewritten as fiction. A lesson that would be passed on to all his protégés at Serpent's Tail: if you want to write the truth, sometimes its necessary to write fiction. That the recent IPCC investigation of those police involved in the Lynette White case collapsed in January 2012 only goes to underscore this point.

Williams next foray was not pure inventiveness either. Published in 1997 but set between 1981 and 84, *Faithless* was a further application of the methodology of memory and place. A smart noir about how the ambitious Eighties stole up on the idealistic dreams of the Seventies, it opens with a sublime evocation of Camden's old main drag and the generation who *came of age in the years between punk and Thatcher. Squatters and punks, all in bands, all at home on this dirty stretch of high street, with its one run-down dance-hall turned rock'n'roll flea-pit, its hippy bookshop and record store, its miserable Irish pubs and grisly cafés.*

*And now,* goes on his narrator Jeff, *I was looking at what we'd done to it. Driven out the butcher, the baker and the Indian grocer, lost the locksmith, the fishmonger and the TV repair shop. Dismantled the Co-Op, the printers and the Halal shop. Replaced them all with leather jacket shops and multi-coloured Dr Martens emporia, the youth culture capital of Europe, the marketplace of cool.*

At the beginning of the novel, Jeff catches a glimpse of a girl he was once involved with, back in the early Eighties. As an example of that loop of time I was talking about earlier, re-reading the novel now, there is something about her that makes the hairs stand up on the back of the neck.

> She wore boxing boots from Lonsdales and called herself a boy's name to prove it. She was tall and dark. Wore black tights, had her hair in a ponytail, rockabilly style. Big almond eyes, jet-black hair. Italian, I supposed, going by her name. She was North London anyway.

Turns out, she's Jewish North London. Her name, like that of Amy Winehouse's first album, is Frank. Is it a ghost of Camden Town's past or its future, that Jeff sees, reflected through the glass of Burger King's window, disappearing into the night?

Whichever, Williams' mediumistic abilities to predict the future of crime fiction remained unerringly accurate with his signing for Serpent's Tail of the Galway writer Ken Bruen in 1996. Like Derek Raymond, Bruen was a man with an itinerant past, who had worked as a security guard on the Twin Towers, and as a foreign language teacher in Vietnam and South America, where he endured a life-altering three-month incarceration in a Brazilian jail.

Bruen had been the first in his family to attend university — he gained a PhD in Metaphysics at Trinity College, Dublin — which was as much an anathema to his parents as Derek Raymond's dereliction of his destiny as a future business leader to the fleshpots of Soho. "The only book in our home was the Bible," Bruen recalled. "My parents forbade books. They thought I needed help because I wanted to be a writer!"

Instead, Bruen wrote crime fiction laced with huge doses of his literary and musical loves, set in the South London streets where he was working as a teacher at the end of the Nineties. *Rilke on Black*, his story of a motley band of kidnappers and their businessman prey was, he once told me, an attempt to get his students to appreciate the poetry of Rainer Maria Rilke by having a suave gangster repeating his lines as a form of Existentialist rap mantra.

He applied the same philosophy to the next year's *Her Last Call to Louis MacNeice*, the tale of a repo man and former bankrobber who falls fatally in love with a poetry addict; and 1997's *The Hackman Blues*, a brutal tango between a gay gangster and a South London crime boss who imagines he looks like the star of *The French Connection*. But there was one character who comes along at the end of *Rilke...* who would go on to take centre stage in what would become Bruen's breakthrough series, the endearingly nihilistic Detective Sergeant Brand.

Like his creator, Brand is an Irish renegade with a drop of bad blood, the rogue gene that Bruen considers saved him from the direst torments of his past. He forms one third of the leading trio of coppers who propel the series that began with *A White Arrest* for The Do-Not Press in 1998.

*R&B they were called*, Bruen expounds. *If Chief Inspector Roberts was like the Rhythm, then Detective Sergeant Brant was the darkest Blues*. WPC Falls is more taken with County and Western, probably because her love life resembles the lyrics of a tear-stained Dolly Parton classic. And no wonder. The villains these three will chase, and often fail to catch, throughout *A White Arrest*, 1999's *Taming The Alien* and 2000's *The McDead* include a serial killer intent on offing the entire England cricket squad and a psychopathic rapist, for whom Falls has to act as bait.

Their beat is a Lambeth/Southwark triangle between Brixton, Oval and The Elephant, bordered by The Cricketer's pub, where, in a former life, No Exit Press' publisher Jim Driver used to book anarcho punk bands, transformed by Bruen into the villainous hub of this manor; Coldharbour Lane, where vigilante gangs plot against the dealers of Railton Road; and The Spirit of Athens Taverna, Walworth Road, where mezze and moonshine are served up by snitches, under the concrete concourse.

Bruen's prose is a heady mixed of the ultra hardboiled familiar from American crime novels and his own, unique and addictive form of non-linear poetry. There are always a supporting cast of itinerants in his tales, *Big Issue* vendors who act as the unseen eyes of the city, with surprising past histories that few, besides Bruen, care to tell. Take this fellow, who appears before DCI Roberts in *The McDead*:

> A mini-cab later and he arrived in Stockwell, where the pitbulls travelled in twos. Ludlow Road is near the tube station, a short mugging away. At that hour the streets were littered with
> the undead
> the lost
> and the frozen.
> The building was a warren of bedsits. No lock on the front door. A wino was spread in the hall, his head came up, wheezed: 'Is it Tuesday?'
> 'No.'
> Roberts wondered if the guy even knew the year but hey... he was going to argue? He said, 'It's Thursday, OK?'
> 'Ah, good. I play golf on Tuesdays.'
> Of course.

Bruen is always careful to tip his hat to the few who have walked this way before. In *A White Arrest* he quotes Patrick Hamilton from 1941, casting his eye back to pre-War London in *Hangover Square*: *"Those whom God deserted are given a room and a gas fire in Earl's Court..."* Then, *"Since Derek Raymond died, so did the characters,"* he notes in *Taming the Alien*.

Both Bruen's and Williams' work would appear in a pivotal tome from 1997. *Fresh Blood II* was edited by

Derek Raymond's former agent and the owner of the now sadly defunct Murder One bookshop, Maxim Jakubowski, and black cab-driving crimewriter Mike Ripley, and also appeared on The Do-Not Press.

This compilation presented the strongest new voices in UK crime fiction at the time, but its stand out contribution didn't come from an adherent to the genre. Iain Sinclair had been tramping the Thames-side routes since the Seventies, weaving history into a trilogy of works that began with the prose poems *Lud Heat* in 1975 and *Suicide Bridge* (1981) then exploded into a fever dream of a novel, *White Chappell, Scarlet Tracings*, in 1987.

During that time, Sinclair had working as a labourer to sustain his writing — cutting grass in East London graveyards, rolling barrels in Truman's Brewery, Brick Lane — and crossing the country in pursuit of rare editions in a supplementary trade as a book dealer. All of which fed into *White Chappell, Scarlet Tracings*. This dense, hallucinogenic triple-narrative conjures the twin spectres of London's most iconic detective and villain: Sherlock Holmes and Jack the Ripper, back to haunt a London shrouded in the shadows and fog of Thatcher's malevolent reign. "In my work," he explained, "the pains of the past need to be appeased — or else they come back."

In one thread, book dealer Nicholas Lane finds a rare edition of *A Study in Scarlet* in a rain-sodden Fenland village and brings it back to London in the hope of turning it into a fortune. In parallel, a century previously, the infant William Gull watches his dead father's Thames barge bearing the cholera-stricken paternal body away — more miasmas coming downriver from the East. Gull becomes an eminent Victorian surgeon, keeper of Royal secrets and clandestine butcher of Whitechapel working girls. The author weaves between these dialogues, following the smell of violets through Hawksmoor churchyards, Farringdon Road bookstalls, the footsteps of Blake's *London*:

> But most thro' midnight streets I hear, he quotes
> How the youthful Harlot's curse
> Blasts the new born Infant's tear,
> And blights with plagues the Marriage hearse

*White Chappell* is cast under the same 'vile psychic weather' as the Factory series and there are many parallels in the work of Raymond and Sinclair. They were friends — Sinclair and his collaborator, the author and filmmaker Chris Petit, put Raymond centre stage in their 1992 film, *The Cardinal and the Corpse* and brought him face to face with his lookalike, the book dealer Nicholas Stone, upon whom *White Chappell*'s Nicholas Lane is based. As a book dealer, Sinclair became familiar with those authors of the Thirties and Forties whom Raymond revered — and has recently played a large part in reviving interest in new editions of books by Alexander Baron, James Curtis and Gerald Kersh by Black Spring Press, Five Leaves and London Books.

In *Fresh Blood II*, Sinclair looked back to a more recent East End past to summon a prophecy for the future of crime fiction. *No More Yoga of the Night Club*, named after a Jah Wobble song, centres the doomed figure of Jack the Hat McVitie, the gangster murdered by Reggie Kray, a man from the world of Derek Raymond's youth, which Sinclair encapsulates thus:

> Old Etonian chancers sharing a half with dysfunctional psychopaths, blisters on their knuckles. Taffeta crooners talking horseflesh with bent peers. Gangsters trading rent boys with unfrocked cabinet ministers.

Sinclair's Jack steams through this world on a narcotic bender, throwing abuse and ashtrays at Dorothy Squires, knocking off bookies, calling Ronald Kray a fairy in front of his assembled firm. As the author contests, he wills his own death, ends up doomed to spend each night ever after as a shade, endlessly repeating his last night on earth through the myriad cracked mirrors of unreliable memory.

In his introduction to the piece, Sinclair expounds further on his interest in the Kray Twins and their circle. He concludes that the whole era is in need of revisiting, but that: *"It needs a James Ellroy to take hold of them, to shape a narrative from the brutal farce of their paranoid monologues."*

Enter Jake Arnott. An escapee from Aylesbury, a bright grammar school boy who fled from his father's aspirations of a middle management future and ended up working as a mortuary assistant in University College Hospital, London. An adolescent struggling with conflicting sexual impulses, he came out as bisexual in his twenties and, inspired by his grandmother, a former Soho showgirl, followed her muse to the radical Red Ladder theatrical troupe in Leeds. An angry young man of punk vintage who served time in South London squatland, involved on what he looks back on as: "endless marches, demos and meetings".

Who better to seize that narrative and, over the course of three breathtakingly brilliant books, follow its course through three decades of epic pop history until the crimes of Reg and Ron became transmogrified into Nineties Lad Mag culture and the caper films of posh boys in search of a bit of rough?

Arnott sets out his stall in the frontispiece of 1999's *The Long Firm*, quoting Bertholt Brecht from *The Threepenny Opera*: 'What's breaking into a bank compared with founding one?' Harry Starks, the central figure this bold as brassknuckles début was cast partly from Brecht's aspirational villain Macheath and partly from Ron Kray: a homosexual gangster who yearns to turn his rackets into legitimate business and join the ranks of his empire heroes, T.E. Lawrence and Winston Churchill; a blackmail artist working his way up through MPs and businessmen with similar sexual proclivities that can be usefully exploited; a man who is once at ease with his gayness and in no mind to have it legalised. And a bitter disappointment to his father, a Communist East End Jew who once led the charge against Oswald Mosley's Blackshirts on Cable Street.

The verisimilitude of the parallel universe he creates is down to Arnott's outsider eye for the tiny detail, the clandestine codes that will unlock the metaphorical green door into the secret worlds beyond. This is how, seen through the eyes of *The Long Firm*'s first narrator, would-be wide-boy Terry, Harry makes his entrance to The Casbah Lounge coffee shop, to the haunting strains of John Leyton's *Johnny Remember Me*:

> A group of Earl's Court Queens were there with cheap Polari sophistication. Vada this, vada that. Casual bitchiness judging by anybody's fleeting object of affection.
>
> Then he came in. Thick set in a dark suit and tightly knotted tie. Looking out of place amidst all the loud clothes the young homos were sporting. Standing out sombre and heavy among the bright shirts and hipster slacks from Vince or Lord John. He looked around the coffee bar, negotiating all the signals, all the brief flashes of eye contact with a weary frown as if his imposing presence was a burden. He looked clumsy and awkward, intimidated for all his toughness. All the looks, the staring. In places he was more used to, spielers, drinking clubs, heavy boozers like the Blind Beggar or the Grave Maurice, that level of eyeballing would have seemed an affront, a prelude to combat. Here, he had to get used to the fierce looks and learn a new way of staring. He had to come off guard in order to make contact.

Arnott takes a similar microscope to his second narrator, dissolute MP Teddy Thursby, a dead ringer for the late Lord Robert Boothby. Like James Ellroy, Arnott shapes events from a history obscured by smart lawyers. In real life, when the *Daily Mirror* got wind of Boothby's amorous associations with Ron Kray, Harold Wilson's 'Mr Fixit' and later Lord Chancellor, Arnold Goodman MP, offered to represent the Tory peer in a libel action which resulted in an apology from the paper and a pay-out for libel that put the kybosh on any similar claims from Fleet Street. This cross-party co-operation is perhaps explained in *The Long Firm*, when, shortly after receiving his title, Thursby is introduced to Harry by the staggeringly indiscreet Labour MP Tom Driberg, who takes him to a party in Harry's Chelsea flat.

To reciprocate Harry's hospitality, Teddy takes him to White's, the oldest gentleman's club in London, correctly deducing that: *It retains a touch of aristocratic raffishness that has all but vanished from the rest of clubland, a quality that I instinctively knew Harry would be drawn to.* Teddy recounts in his diary:

> Harry leant back in his leather armchair, taking a sip of brandy & soda, casually surveying the fixtures & fittings.
> 'Nice place,' he commented, 'wouldn't mind joining myself.'
> I smiled, hoping he was joking.

Joining Terry and Thursby in this caper is actress Ruby Ryder, a Rank Charm School starlet with a touching similarity to Barbara Windsor, who marries one of Harry's gang, cat burglar Eddie Doyle. Ruby becomes Starks' beard when Eddie goes away for a stretch in Wandsworth, helping Harry transform his Stardust Club from Soho showbiz dive to raunchy revue bar as the sex industry creeps into those streets known to cabbies as the Dirty Dozen.

But bursting through the middle of the book, with his trousers round his ankles and a pork pie hat covering his shame, is the realisation of Iain Sinclair's prophecy: Jack the Hat McVitie rides again. It starts like this:

> Soho Square. Park the cream and blue Mark II Zodiac and walk around to The Flamingo on Wardour Street. Mod club. Spade music blaring out below the pavement. R&B. Soul, they call it. Tip some hat brim at the doorman and slip him a note with a sly grin. In. Downstairs. Check the nag in the inside suit pocket. Pills. All kinds. Purple hearts, French blues, nigger minstrels, black bombers. Enough to keep those mod boys and girls dancing all night to that spade music...

New record starts. Needle scratch static. Engine noise. Rat-tat-tat-tat gunfire. Car tyres squealing. Crash. A lairy spade voice mouths off. AL CAPONE'S GUNS DON'T ARGUE.

In *The Long Firm*, Jack is ducking and diving between The Krays, The Richardsons and Starks' ganglands of the Wild East, Sinister South and Way Out West End; spinning and weaving between youth cultures as he doles out doobs to the modernists and their descendants — hippies in Hampstead who medicine him back with a near-fatal dose of self-realisation in the form of an acid tab; and baldheads, as he dubs the adherents of this new ska sound, revealed to Jack by his youthful accomplice, Beardsley. Fittingly, in this shifting, cross-pollinating underworld London, Jamaican singer Prince Buster's ode to Prohibition-era Chicago's top boss is the soundtrack to McVitie's mad, spiralling descent. Which finishes up like this:

> Up the steps to the front door and in. Soul music coming up from the basement. Go downstairs. Chicka, chicka, chicka.
> 'Where's the party?' I say. 'Jack's here. Where's all the booze? Where are all the birds?'
> Go into the basement room. No birds. No booze. Just a couple of boys dancing together. Fat Ron sitting on a sofa watching them. Leering. Toad-like eyes blink over me. Reg is behind me. Pulls out a gun. Cold metal against my head.
> You've got it coming to you, Jack the Hat.
> 'Do him!' Ron hisses.

*The Long Firm* ends with the confessions of a fifth character, self-styled radical criminologist Lenny, whose spell teaching at Long Marsh Prison makes a star pupil out of Harry Starks, incarcerated since 1969, the dark, implosive end of a decade. Now it's 1979, and Lenny's world is tilting on its axis just as Harry's did, the certainties of free love curtailed when his long-suffering girlfriend takes up with his student bit on the side, his proto-punk pupils sneering at his hippy long hair and the paper he has spent a decade researching thoroughly intellectually trashed by the criminal he's been studying. When Harry makes an audacious jailbreak, Lenny crosses the divide and becomes his accomplice, helping Harry abscond across the sea to Morocco. Arnott pursues the link between the social upheavals of the Sixties into the inflammatory politics of the Seventies and Eighties in his next book, 2001's *He Kills Coppers*.

He opens on another key cultural flashback: London 1966, the summer of England's World Cup Victory. We are back in West End Central police station, getting a taste of what forged Derek Raymond's fictitious Factory through the eyes of newly promoted detective Frank Taylor:

> West End Central, Savile Row. C Division. Crowded Crime Room briefing. Nipper Read out front giving the spiel. Clampdown on vice in Soho. Reinforcements drafted in to swamp the patch. Subtle hints: West End Central needs a bit of a clean-up itself. The area has a reputation — nasty rumours about officers on the take. Newly appointed DCI Nipper wants to change all that, apparently.

Taylor's cynical appraisal of the man who would take down the Kray Twins and his infringement on the well-organised crime of the Soho Vice Squad sets the tone of conflicted masculinity that will follow. Taylor is self-described as 'a little bit bent for the job'. After all, unlike his scrupulous best friend Dave Thomas, still plodding round the dull beat of Shepherd's Bush, Frank wants to get on. But it's in Shepherd's Bush that Taylor's destiny awaits.

Meanwhile, tabloid reporter Tony Meehan is chasing another story. Dazzled by Truman Capote's *In Cold Blood*, he makes an unsuccessful attempt to solicit Ronnie Kray's memoirs, in a meeting set up by his louche young friend, Julian. Tony has more than a passing interest in the mechanics of the criminal mind — he has his own secret life as a psychopathic killer, brief spells of murderous frenzy punctuate his tightly-contained existence, indeed, he will later end up smothering the ageing Teddy Thursby in order to get his hands on the peer's explosive diaries.

After being knocked back by The Colonel, he unwillingly follows Julian across town to Notting Hill and an audience of a different kind. Here are new worlds colliding:

> It was in the basement of a bookshop on Kensington Park Road. A motley crew assembled — beards, beads, multi-coloured clothes, peace sign badges. Everyone talking about Utopia, Peace, Liberation, Revolution, Love. God did they go on about Love. Julian and I both stood out as being the only people in the room with short hair and ordinary clothes. I guessed they must have thought us real squares... This bunch of well spoken hippies liked to call themselves freaks, as if it were something glamorous and bohemian. As if they had any idea what horror it was to be a real freak.
> We went for a drink afterwards. Henekey's on Portobello Road. It was full of freaks.
> 'Not very beautiful, are they?' I commented. 'The Beautiful People.'

Interestingly, this bookshop is based on a real life enterprise of artist Brian Catling, who would later escort Iain Sinclair around the Ripperlands of *White Chappell, Scarlett Tracings*. A tipping of an old pork pie hat, perhaps. Back in *He Kills Coppers*, a vengeful Tony decides to set up a drugs bust in Henekey's the following weekend. Which puts him first on the spot when three policemen, among them Frank Taylor's best mate Dave Thomas, are gunned down near Wormwood Scrubs prison by a trio of small-time crooks led by an ex-serviceman called Billy Porter.

Arnott's fictitious Porter is based on Harry Roberts, who remains incarcerated for the crimes he committed in the summer of 1966, one of the UK's longest-serving criminals. Roberts had done his National Service for the British Army on two bloody mid-Fifties fronts — the Kenya Emergency, or Mau-Mau Uprising as it was then called, and the guerrilla war fought between the Malayan Liberation Army and Commonwealth forces. It was in the jungles of Malaya that Roberts claimed to have 'acquired a taste for killing', a scenario Arnott re-imagines for his fictitious Porter.

But, following the shootings, Porter's path diverges dramatically from Roberts'. Arnott's Billy gets away, and using the survival skills learned from the army, remains undetected for long enough to establish a new life for himself working on fairgrounds, the fringes of the gypsy life and the nascent travelling community of the early Seventies, changing his identity to that of Mick, who paints fairground rides. But Frank Taylor hasn't forgotten him. Neither has Tony, who, now scripting Murder Monthlies for a lowly part-work publisher, re-imagines his *In Cold Blood* as the investigation that will lead to Porter's capture. And neither have the football hooligans who sing his name as they mash each other up on the terraces to the tune of *London Bridge is Falling Down*:

> Billy Porter is our friend, is our friend, is our friend/
> Billy Porter is our friend/He kills coppers.

Still living as Mick, and involved with a group of peace protesters, Billy Porter himself doesn't hear this chant until a 1985 demo at Greenham Common. An altercation follows, that leads him back London in the company of some budding anarchists who have no idea who Mick really is. Neither can Mick much recognise this London from the one he left in 1966:

> A whole square of houses had been taken over by squatters... The half-derelict houses had been reno-

vated in a haphazard way. Windows fixed with what was at hand, plumbing improvised, front doors painted garishly in a bricolage of occupation. There were graffiti on the walls: NO CRUISE, MEAT IS MURDER, STOP THE CITY, EAT THE RICH — strange, apocalyptic warnings.

Using his skills as a painter and decorator, Mick secures cash-in-hand work renovating old warehouses in Docklands as the city shapeshifts into Margaret Thatcher's vision. Here, he witnesses the end of another era:

> There was a big demonstration outside the new premises of the *Sunday Illustrated* in Docklands. Mick went along with them. It was quite close to where he worked. A group of young men covered their faces and busied themselves hurling missiles at the police lines. Police in riot gear retaliated, but the stone-throwers were behind the main ranks of the protesters and were able to get away. They're just bloody hooligans, really, Mick thought. And they'd sing that song again. The Billy Porter song. It sent a shiver down his spine.

Time is soon up for Mick, for Billy and for Frank Taylor's dream of confronting the man who stole his best friend's life. But all is not quite lost for murderous Tony Meehan. At the beginning of 1995's *truecrime*, he has got himself a job ghost-writing for The Groombridge Press, publishers of nascent Lad's mag *Sorted*, who have built up an empire trading in celebrity gangster memoirs. His Billy Porter book having been long-since remaindered, he is now interviewing Eddie Doyle, former Harry Starks' associate and erstwhile husband of Ruby Ryder. Eddie has just come out of a 12-stretch for his part in the 1983 Hounslow bullion heist — 15million quids' worth that still remains hidden. Tony, still aching to write his *In Cold Blood*, seizes this link to Harry as a golden opportunity. Meehan captures the mood of Cool Britannia in his usual erudite manner:

True Crime, what a racket it is. I prefer to rearticulate this term into a lower case composite: truecrime. Like George Orwell's newspeak words thoughtcrime or sexcrime... True and Crime, words that were once at odds with each other as much as alibi and detection, now conspire to create trashy bestsellers.

*truecrime*'s most compelling character is Julie, the daughter of another Starks associate, Big Jock McClusky, gunned down at Harry's Spanish hideaway at the end of *The Long Firm*. Masquerading as Julie Kincaid, she has tried to bury the traumas of her past by following her former Stardust showgirl mother's dream of being an actress. But, when her trustafarian boyfriend Jez, and his best mate Piers, the editor of *Sorted*, start work on a screenplay called *Scrapyard Bulldog*, she finds herself conspiring with them as a way of confronting her ghosts. Julie nails the whole mid-Nineties, *Lock, Stock and Two Smirking Barrels* epoch with her observations on the men-only first draft of Jez's script:

> An absence of women was merely part of the absence of any sense of consequence to the actions in the screenplay. It was a complete parody of what had afflicted my life. Violence rendered as slapstick, tragedy made comic. One big joke, ugly and mocking. But there was something quite brilliant about it as well. It struck me that this was what so many people thought about men like my dad. Jez had got something. The laughter of cruelty. But I'd have the last laugh, I thought.

Then there is the man through whose eyes we see the decades unfurl. A protégé of Jack the Hat's old sidekick, Beardsley, Mile End boy made good Gaz Kelly has been living the high-life as a drug-dealing, door security firm provider — until the break-up of his marriage tailspins into a bad deal and two dead men in a Range Rover on the Essex marshes holding all his cash.

Gaz has been working with Beardsley since the Seventies. His frequent incarcerations and subsequent attempts to reintegrate in a world that has changed beyond his comprehension each time provide the book's richest comedy material. When he comes out his first long stretch in 1982, Gaz is still wearing the skinhead threads that were de rigueur with his InterCity Firm comrades two years previously. Now he gets cruised by a gay man wearing the same clobber. It is the hooligans who are wearing pastel knitwear and Italian designer shirts.

*Poofs dressed as hooligans, hooligans dressed like poofs. Well, I thought, I'd seen it all now*, he recounts. But he hasn't. London changes before Gaz's incredulous eyes many times again. Next it is the rave scene, M25 parties arranged on pagers by enterprising young toff, Ben Holroyd Carter. Getting wind of the money to be made out of pills, Beardsley's crew soon see off Ben HB. But the next time Gaz claps eyes on him, Ben has an empire — The Groove Corporation, run out of a converted warehouse on the docks, and is on his way to Number 10 for champagne with Tony Blair.

As Soho is cleaned up and Old Compton Street given a makeover, Gaz ends up comparing at the Comedy Club, the latest incarnation of the Starlight. Through this, he starts getting bit part work as an actor, ends up taking one of the leads in *Scrapyard Bulldog*, and the world of celebrity opens up before him.

For the characters of *truecrime*, London's past comes full circle. Using Thursby's diaries as a treasure map, Tony Meehan and Eddie Doyle locate the lost gold bullion — under the concrete of a disused dockside warehouse. Julie, having used her mother's connection with Ruby Ryder to hire Eddie as a consultant on *Scrapyard Bulldog* and subsequently fallen in love with him, uses the warehouse as a location for the film's final scene — and a lure to bring her nemesis Harry Starks back to London. Tony, having screwed up royally the deal he had with Groombridge press for Eddie's memoirs, ends up writing Gaz's biography instead as his penance.

And Arnott weaves in a touching send off to Ronnie Kray and the passing of the old East End into themepark designerland:

> A monster's funeral, the churchyard teeming with old lags and young wannabes. A phalanx of bouncers, the cream of London's doormen, formed a guard of dishonour around the lich-gate. A police helicopter buzzed overhead. The hearse arrived. A black-and-gold, glass-sided carriage, drawn by six black-plumed horses. Victoriana kitsch, just as he would have wanted. The Last Empire Hero. Wreaths and flowered tributes to the grand old psychopath: RON and THE COLONEL. One from Reggie, his womb-mate: THE OTHER HALF OF ME, like a floral expression of schizophrenia.

It was the old East End that brought us our next writer, who grew up one road away from Cable Street and spent a childhood ensconced in Whitechapel library. But the stories this writer grew up to bring us are an insight into a very different terrain. Dreda Say Mitchell, the daughter of *Windrush* Generation immigrants from Grenada, is the first to tell the secret history of London from a West Indian perspective.

Mitchell's life was shaped by typically wayward impulses. A star athlete as a schoolgirl, she shocked her teachers by quitting sport to follow academia. As she recalled, she didn't want to be channelled into the expected avenues of black youth within the education system. Instead, she determined to proceed to the School of African and Oriental Studies and take a degree in African history. A career as a teacher and head-teacher followed. Then Mitchell began to feel her younger self calling back to her from within those library shelves. She started shaping a story, set on a mirror image of the Estate where she grew up.

*Running Hot*, Mitchell's 2004 début, evinced a very different gangland to the one we left at St Matthew's, Bethnal Green. This is Dalston Junction, seven years after the Colonel's funeral:

Mehmet Ali lay in east London's number one outdoor spot to die. He lay two doors down from Kwame's Hotshot Barbers and three doors up from Rosaman's Cabs. Over him rocked the bodies of two men as they stomped, twisted and sliced their shoe heels into him. An hour earlier his attackers had been jerking their bodies to the pounding energy of Judge Dredd's Nightsound. Now they continued their dance.... After they had found him, as they knew they would, they'd dragged him to Cinnamon Junction, right on the main road. They had known that this spot was too notorious, too in-your-face, for any of the cars passing on Monday at 2.23a.m. to stop and help. Anyway, any car cruising the Junction at that time of morning had its own business to attend to.

This is the story of 29-year-old Elijah 'Schoolboy' Hammond, who dreams of escape from Ernest Bevin House and the surrounding streets, where, *treading on someone's footwear could mean being permanently taken out of this life...* Knives are on Schoolboy's mind as the book opens. Chef's knives. The offer he's been made to apprentice at restaurant in Devon is conditional on him turning up with the proper kit.

Opportunity presents itself outside Cinnamon Junction, when he stumbles over the body of Mehmet Ali — and picks up a mobile lying by the corpse. If Schoolboy can convert the phone into the £40 he needs, he can be on the first West Coast Mainline out of there. Trouble is, the mobile is the connection between two rival gangs. What follows is a hyperadrenalised rush through seven days in the streets of Hackney's murder mile as Schoolboy shadowboxes his way between his pursuers to get to Paddington station with his knives in hand. Winner of the 2004 Crime Writers Association Début Dagger, *Running Hot* was the beginning of an incendiary career for the remarkable Mitchell.

Yet there are haunting echoes in this landscape of a previous novel, set in the socially diverse streets of Hackney in 1963. Written by the late Alexander Baron and recently republished by Black Spring Press, *The Lowlife* tells the story of Jewish chancer Harryboy Boas, and the life he lives between Ingrams Terrace — *part of a street that joins Stoke Newington High Street next to Amhurst Road, not far north of Dalston junction* — and the dog tracks of White City and Walthamstow.

To Harryboy, brought up in the same streets as Mitchell at the time Harry Starks' father was fighting Mosley's Blackshirts, *Hackney isn't the East End. It's the mark of the outsider, when you hear someone call Hackney the East End.*

But Harryboy's own community has scattered since the War, drifted North from Bethnal Green and Aldgate, so he is very much an outsider in this land too. Here is how he describes the streets around Dalston Junction in the early Sixties:

> All is quiet and decent. Negroes have come to live, more every month. And Cypriots. The Negroes are of marvellous respectability. Every Sunday morning they all go to the Baptist Church in the High Street. You should see the men, in beautiful pearl grey suits and old fashioned trilbies with curled brims, the big women full of dignity, and the little girls in white muslin and bonnets. It slays me. They are the Victorian residents of this street, come back a century later, with black skins. And the Cypriots — they gather at their gates, throwing their children in the air and kissing them when they come down. The people in Ingrams Terrace don't mix but they all say good morning to each other. I never smelt any hatred between one kind and another, not even an ember that might flare up in the future.

Just how sadly wrong Harryboy's prediction would turn out to be is laid bare in Dreda Say Mitchell's next novel, 2007's epoch-straddling *Killer Tune*, which tells the parallel stories of upcoming young rapper Lord Tribulation, LT for short, and his father King Stir It Up, a veteran musician who came up through the sound systems and radical politics of the Seventies. The crime at the centre of the book, which ripples out thirty years from 1976, emanates from a house in the fictitious, but etymologically loaded, Cecil Rhodes Square, slap bang in the middle of Harryboy's former manor.

Like Schoolboy Hammond before him, LT lives in Ernest Bevin House. As the book opens, he is teetering on the brink of a life-changing record deal, while his father, The King, languishes in hospital, nearing the end of his own days, being interviewed by a young journalist about the history of the Notting Hill Carnival, and in particular, the riots of 1976. The King doesn't get to answer her question — he is distracted by the scene unfurling outside his window. A black youth, wearing a du-rag in a deliberate imitation of LT's trademark style, has just launched a Molotov cocktail at the Victorian house opposite.

The journalist doesn't get to repeat it either. Shortly after witnessing this incident, The King gets a phonecall and absconds from hospital. His body is found in a back alleyway in Hoxton — an area of the city he vowed he would never set foot in. In the aftermath of this, and the storm of controversy about potential links between his music and the firebombing incident, LT is compelled to investigate the circumstances of his father's suspicious demise — assisted by the journalist, Bernie Ray, who turns out to be his long-lost girlfriend.

Like Derek Raymond's *He Died With His Eyes Open*, the murdered man has left the clues to finding his assailants on a series of tape recordings. Which tell a whole alternate history of London and what happened to those regal Victorian Negroes in the years since Harryboy moved out of the East End improper.

In the book's most chilling passage, we get to find out why The King despised Hoxton. After a day at the Notting Hall Carnival in 1984, he and LT got stranded on the wrong side of Commercial Road to be after hours. It is a landscape picked out, like Jake Arnott's, with a minutiae of contemporary detail:

...they reached the intersection where Shoreditch High Street becomes Kingsland Road. Suddenly the pressure of the King's hand pulled LT back. Made him stop. As if the King was stopping them both from crossing into a minefield... It was some years later that LT realised that crossing that street meant they were going to be entering what locals called The Hate Estate. The south-west of Hackney that ran from Hoxton to Haggerston and threaded through Brick Lane and Bethnal Green was the homeland of the National Front... They moved quickly, walking swiftly past a GEORGE DAVIS IS INNOCENT slogan painted in white on the wall. They kept moving. For one minute. Three minutes. Five minutes later they left the darkness of the bridge behind them and reached the open road again. They hit the bend where Falkirk Street touches the main road on its left. That was when they heard the voices. Male, boisterous, singing, with the crude aroma of alcohol in the main melody. He could not make out the words of their song, but the acoustics of The Hate Estate told them they were coming from Haggerston, across the road...

The trail that King Stir It Up has left for LT leads back to the square where the firebombing took place, and the Seventies headquarters of the Liberation Republic, a movement with parallels to the Hackney Black People's Association and further echoes of Michael X's Black House in Holloway Road. This was the story retold in John Williams' 2008 biography *Michael X*, that can be read in tandem with *Killer Tune* for further insight into the history of race, sex and class through the shifting personae of one mixed-race man in London from the Fifties to the Seventies.

In Mitchell's parallel universe, the Liberation Republic is discovered by The King after a night spent in the cells of the Unity Road police station — nicknamed The Abomination — which acts as a metaphor for several actual stations in the district and London's troubling history of relations between police and the black community, from the death of Colin Roach in the custody of Stoke Newington police on January 1983 right up to the shooting of Mark Duggan by Operation Trident officers in August 2011.

The King's cell-mate is a man nicknamed Houdini, for reasons that soon become clear: he has a lawyer spring the two of them in double quick time. Intrigued by both the man and the community group he comes from, The King is drawn into their world, which, rather like Michael X's Racial Adjustment Advancement Society, is not exactly all it seems. LT discovers a legacy clandestine collusion between mainstream politicians and one-time radicals, that feeds off fear and misunderstanding within the very communities they are supposed to represent.

As in Ken Bruen's *White Trilogy* and Jake Arnott's London cycle, Mitchell's streets are alive with the sound of music. *Killer Tune* grooves a history of the city through the beats fashioned within its streets and the hopes and dreams of the people who made them, fusing pop culture with real events and their ever-attendant supporting feature, urban legend.

Which brings me, finally, to a pair of detectives who have seen all of these London stories unfold — and more besides. In the books of Christopher Fowler, Arthur Bryant and John May are veterans of the Metropolitan Police's clandestine Peculiar Crimes Unit, set up during the Second World War to tackle crimes of a politically sensitive nature, or those liable to cause social upheaval.

It was, as their now acting head Raymond Land discusses in a secret memo to Whitehall...*a time of desperation when... a great many experimental ideas were proposed by the Churchill government, including the employment of Dennis Wheatley, the horror-story writer, as a member of the war cabinet.* Six decades later, no single government has yet been able to disband the operation.

Fowler's octogenarian detectives are outsiders working under the cover — and frequently right up the noses — of the Establishment. Bryant, the perennial scruff with boiled sweets and worse stuck to his pockets, has a head full of arcane historical detail and snouts that include a coven of white witches. May, urbane in a Savile Row suit, is the man of reason constantly adapting to the ever-changing Capital around him, embracing new technology and tapping up rogue computer hackers for tips.

Aided by Diana Dors-lookalike Detective Sergeant Janice Longbright, and a revolving cast of disgruntled ex-coppers, malevolent civil servants, unruly pathologists and star-crossed detectives, Bryant and May traverse just about every district of London encountering every class, race and persuasion of the city's dwellers on their way. Each case is loaded with Fortean facts and secret histories, including the location of the PCU's base, which for the majority of the series is run out of a decaying office on the floor above Mornington Crescent tube station — recalling both the cult game on Radio 4's *I'm Sorry I Haven't a Clue;* and the lodgings of the Victorian artist Walter Sickert. Mornington Crescent the game is shrouded in mysterious origins and obscure rules. Sickert is a man on whom infamy has been pinned.

His *Camden Town Murder* sequence, painted in rooms adjacent to the station, was inspired by the crimes of Jack the Ripper. A hundred years later, American crime writer Patricia Cornwell spent a fortune acquiring these paintings and subjecting them to modern forensic analysis to try and prove Sickert actually *was* Saucy Jack. Though her 2002 book, *Jack The Ripper: Case Closed* was ridiculed by Ripperologists on publication, Fowler's books excel in exposing such links. That he subverts the format of the so-called Golden Age of Thirties crime fiction in the telling of them only strengthens their charm. Agatha Christie's Hercule Poirot might never have tangled with the Leicester Square Vampire, the Deptford Demon or a Highwayman loose in Clerkenwell — but Dennis Wheatley's Duc de Richleau might.

Fowler himself was denied the pleasure of reading as a child. His Green Carnation Award-winning memoir *Paperboy* describes a dreary early existence in 1950s Greenwich, blighted by a tyrannical father who regularly exploded with rage at the idea of his son being '*made out of paper*'. Fowler Snr's reading matter was, apparently, limited to a volume about bomb making. Junior rebelled by reading everything — from cornflake packets to *War and Peace*, which he declaimed to his pet tortoise.

By the age of 24, Fowler had his own film company, Creative Partnership, set up to fill the void left by Hammer Studios and because Fowler was bored of his previous job as an advertising copywriter. Four years later, he moved the company to America, and, getting bored again by the long stretches between jobs, he tried his hand at writing short stories. Luckily, he had a good neighbour in the horror writer Clive Barker, who passed on Fowler's début short story collection to his editor, and a successful, genre-straddling career as a horror, sci fi and crime writer began.

London is a presence in most of Fowler's work, but it is with Bryant and May that his encyclopaedic knowledge — and thirst to know more — about the city runs rampant. Perhaps my favourite of all is 2008's *The Victoria Vanishes*, which delves into those cornerstones of London life most beloved of thirsty writers: pubs.

It begins with the seemingly impossible. After attending a wake, a slightly worse for wear Arthur Bryant is weaving a course back to Mornington Crescent from Charing Cross Road. Slipping into Argyle Walk, a slender alley tucked behind Euston Road, he finds a tiny part of London that has never revealed itself to him before. It all seems remarkably well preserved. He notes:

> ...a pale keystone over a door, initials entwined in a county badge... a carved blind window... perhaps... bricked in because of William III's window tax... a cast-iron railing of daisies and ivy leaves, one which had survived the mass removal of ironwork during the Second World War...

And finally:

> A corner pub, The Victoria Cross, with a sign above it depicting its namesake, the highest recognition for

bravery in the face of the enemy that could be awarded to any member of the British and Commonwealth armed forces... Beneath the sign were opaque lower windows, gold letters in a spotted mirror panel establishing the types of beers served and foundation date. A deserted bar unit, mirrored and shelved, where bottles of whisky and gin remained in places they had doubtless occupied for decades.

As Bryant observes his surroundings, a middle aged woman stumbles drunkenly across the road, staring up at the pub sign before entering The Victoria, where: *a barman emerged to greet her, appearing like an actor taking his cue on a stage set.*

Bryant dismisses the surreal atmosphere of this tiny thoroughfare, until the woman, 46-year-old Carol Wynley, is discovered dead on the corner where he last saw her just minutes after he had departed it. Bryant and May return to Argyle Walk — to find that The Victoria Cross has vanished. Instead, a convenience store stands on the same spot. Try as they might, the duo cannot find any semblance of the scene Bryant witnessed in the architecture around them.

To compound the mystery, other women appear to have died in similar circumstances — and more are following. Naomi Curtis, collapsed inside the Seven Stars pub, Holborn, Jocelyn Roquesby, inside the Old Bell Tavern in Fleet Street, Joanne Kellerman in the Old Dr Butler's Head by London Wall and Jasmina Sherwin in the beer garden of the Barnsbury, King's Cross. The PCU's investigation becomes one mammoth crawl of London's hostelries and the many societies who meet within them.

Bryant is convinced that the locations of the killings hold the key to the killer's identity. He consults a friend from the British Museum, an expert on the mythology and etymology of London named Dr Harold Masters. Masters not only agrees with this prognosis, he goes one further — the killer's underlying motive is to unpick the very fabric of the nation. *'If you wished to undermine everything we stand for as a people, you could do no better than to damage the institution of the pub'* he expounds, echoing Hilaire Belloc's: *When you have lost your Inns drown your empty selves, for you will have lost the last of England.*

Out there in the night, the killer echoes this thinking through his own interior monologue:

> The cavernous inns of The Strand, the narrow taverns of Holborn, the fake rural hostelries of Chelsea, the brash bars of Soho, each had their own tribes. The lotharios, the jobsworths, the brasses, the bosses, brash drunk kids, braying toffs, swearing workmen, all united by the desperate need for companionship.

The PCU discover many variants of forms on which this desire manifests itself. The Conspiracy Club, which meet upstairs in the Sutton Arms near Smithfield Market; the Phobia Society at the Ship and Shovell off the Strand, and the Grand Order of London Immortals in the Yorkshire Grey in Langham Place. These organisations have one thing in common: the desire to discuss ideas and theories outside the narrow parameters of the *partisan and conservative* mainstream press. The great philosophers of London and their natural nocturnal habitat refused to be controlled or contained — not even by the smoking ban.

At the point that they make a major breakthrough in the case, Bryant and May also discover something new about each other. May's wife Jane, whom Bryant had long believed was dead, is a patient in a mental health institution. Sent mad by the death of their daughter Elizabeth, who was killed by the Leicester Square Vampire on a stake-out engineered by her father. Though the situation is different — May is culpable for the death of his daughter, not his wife — the allusions to Derek Raymond's Detective Sergeant come as a clear homage, another stitch in time.

Though, what finally connects the victims and their killer with Emmanuel Swedenborg, the Cato Street

Conspiracy, the MOD Porton Down and the Blood of Christ — and how those forces conspired to make the Victoria vanish — are mysteries I shall not here reveal. But, as Bryant would say, there is a pattern to everything.

And so, I want to end this talk back at the beginning. We have walked the charter'd streets through many different times and angles, so it only seems appropriate to end with our elder statesmen, Bryant and May standing, as William Blake before them, on a bridge above the charter'd Thames. Where Blake saw the future in the Satanic Mills of the Industrial Revolution that inspired his immortal *Jerusalem*, Christopher Fowler's creations stare back through time, multiple visions of the city refracted through their eyes:

> London, the site of the Guy Fawkes plot, home of Newgate and Bedlam. The tarred heads of Jacobites on spikes at Temple Bar, the Cato Street Conspiracy, the Sidney Street siege, the Gordon Riots and the Lollards. Thomas Blood and the stolen Crown Jewels, the highway robbers John Cottington, Dick Turpin and Moll Cutpurse, John Sayer stabbed in the Mint, Elizabeth Brownrigg torturing her maids, Jack the Ripper, the Krays, Ruth Ellis, Jonathan Wild, Jack Sheppard, the Fenian outrage of 1867, the Dynamite Plot of 1883, the Battle of Stepney, the death of the bomber Nourdin, Charlie Peace, the Mannings, Franz Muller the Railway Murderer, Crippen, Christie and Nilsen, the Tichbourne Claimant, the Smithfield burnings, the crowds at Tyburn Tree, Execution Dock at Wapping, the Ratcliffe Highway murders, the Shooter's Hill executions, the scaffolds and gaols at Southwark, Bridewell, Clerkenwell, Wandsworth, Coldbath Fields, Ludgate, Millbank, Brixton, Holloway, Pentonville, Wormwood Scrubs, Fleet, St George's Fields and the floating prison hulks at Woolwich — an overwhelmingly populous timeline of death, desperation and the damned.
>
> You want to be here, amongst it all.

# Lines of Enquiry
## John Harvey

*Some thoughts on the origins of the contemporary British crime novel, mine and other people's — mostly mine*

Let's start with Lesley Fiedler's pronouncement about the urban American crime novel, in his celebrated *Love and Death in the American Novel*.

> Our essential contribution to the form in the twentieth century is a strange off-shoot of the '30s novel of urban violence: a 'realistic' exposé of corruption in the big city, presided over by the private eye. But the private eye is not the dandy turned sleuth; he is the cowboy adapted to life on the city streets, the embodiment of innocence moving untouched through universal guilt. As created by Dashiell Hammett, the blameless shamus is also the honest proletarian, illuminating by contrast the decadent society of the rich.[1]

And, indeed, one of those family trees such as music journalist Pete Frame used to devise for rock bands, might believably trace a line that would progress from the likes of Jack London, Upton Sinclair and the sadly unsung Jim Tully[2], via Hemingway, (the Chicago of this network) to James M. Cain, Horace McCoy and Dashiell Hammett on thus to Raymond Chandler and beyond.

So where's the similar line emanating from British writers of the 30s, leading from pre-war social realism to its post-war variations, crime fiction, the tough, urban kind, included, and where does it extend?

I'm thinking, on the one hand, of such working class novels as Walter Greenwood's *Love on the Dole* (1933), set amongst the poverty-stricken unemployed of Salford, and then, perhaps, Frank Tilsley's *Plebeian Progress* (also 1933) or the later *Champion Road* (1948). Then, moving closer to the subject matter and milieu of crime fiction, there is Gerald Kersh, in particular his 1938 novel, *Night and the City*, and the Patrick Hamilton of *Hangover Square* and *Twenty Thousand Streets Under the Sky*. Less well-known, but recently reissued, Simon Blumenfeld's *Jew Boy* (1935), John Sommerfield's *May Day* (1936) and Robert Westerby's *Wide Boys Never Work* (1937) all explore a sleazy and violent London underworld that reaches from the East End to Soho. And then there are the novels of James Curtis, such as *The Gilt Kid* (1936) and *They Drive By Night* (1938), which come closest to crime fiction as we might most readily understand it.

Does any possible influence they may have had go underground perhaps, to resurface later, or does it wither on the vine, the flinty, some might say arid soil of British crime fiction in the post-war years not exactly receptive to these often violent representations of predominantly working class lives?

As Peter Messent says in his recent survey of Crime Fiction, "... hard-boiled fiction was (primarily) an American form of writing, dating from the late 1920s and 1930s, that offered much more of an explicit challenge to the social and political status quo than its (mainly British) classical detective counterpart."[3]

And one could argue that the fundamentally conservative tradition of the so-called Golden Age, as exemplified by Agatha Christie, Conan Doyle, Dorothy L. Sayers, Ngaio Marsh *et al*, was so all-pervading that the influence of American hard-boiled, vernacular fiction on British crime fiction was kept at bay until well into the 1950s and 60s and even beyond. Expert commentators such as Barry Forshaw and Mike Ripley might be able to point to examples that would shoot a few ragged holes in this argument, but my own, admittedly patchy, reading suggests that with a few exceptions — Marjorie

Allingham's 1952 novel, *The Tiger in the Smoke* being one — the hegemony of the classical tradition in British crime writing — and publishing — throughout this period was largely unchallenged.

In the updated edition of *Dockers and Detectives*, his study of British working class reading and writing, Ken Worpole claims a strong connection between a wide range of American writers including Hammett and Chandler, Steinbeck and Salinger on a number of writers he sees as contributing to "the new wave of working-class realism which broke across British culture in the late 1950s and early 1960s.

> "... the great narrative and stylistic caesura which separates their writing from that of socialist novelists of the pre-war period, such as Howard Fast and Frank Tilsley, for example, could not have been resolved in British writing without the direct influence of the American realist tradition."[4]

The works that Worpole instances in this connection include Brendan Behan's *Borstal Boy* and Frank Norman's *Bang to Rights* (both 1958, both autobiographies) and Alan Sillitoe's novel of the same year, *Saturday Night and Sunday Morning*. To which one might add the early work of Stan Barstow, Keith Waterhouse, Barry Hines and others.

Whether this influence was as direct as Worpole suggests is, I think, open to question, as would be an attempt to claim influence from those earlier British writers mentioned in my opening paragraph.

Take Sillitoe, for instance. Spending his formative years in Nottingham, it would be a not unreasonable assumption that he would have read and been influenced by the early D.H. Lawrence, the short stories in particular, but though aware of Lawrence, he seems to have considered him the end of a line and what he was doing something different and new. Amongst English writers, the only one he claimed to have strongly influenced by was Robert Tressell, whose acknowledged classic of working class literature, *The Ragged Trousered Philanthropists*, was published in 1914. In general, he felt most English writers were too parochial and looked, for inspiration, not to Hemingway or Steinbeck, but towards Dostoyevsky and Camus and the picaresque Spanish novelists of the 16th and early 17th centuries.

Where Worpole is spot on, of course, is when he points to a new wave, a sea change that gathered momentum towards the end of the '50s and then swept through British culture and society in the 1960s. And, as one who was on hand, I can say, with feeling, not before time.

All right, I know there were the Festival of Britain and the Goon Show and Ealing Studios, but really ... I mean, it was safe, but it was kind of dull, moribund: a world still in the shadow of the ration book and the Blitz. How does J.G. Ballard characterise it in his memoir, *Miracles of Life*?[5] A world in which we were taught to "show respect to one's elders, never be too keen, take it on the chin." A world that encouraged "second rateness and low expectations."

Only towards the end of the 50s did this consensus start to break down to the sound of Elvis Presley and (for God's sake!) Bill Haley and the Comets, the sight of James Dean up there on the screen, and the upsurge of young people from all over the country going away (usually as far away as they could) to university; all of this contributing to a fracturing of the status quo that came from a new class awareness, the steady upsurge of regionalism, the decline of censorship and the broadening of the parameters of permissible sexual behaviour. The newly evolving Britain that would give us Arthur Seaton, Joe Lampton and Billy Liar.

Novels and autobiography aside, the other area Worpole pinpoints as significant in carrying on the tradition of working class writing, is drama — drama of all kinds. And here, at last, but exceptionally, there seems to be a clearly traceable line leading from the '30s and '40s to the post-war years and beyond.

Alexander Baron, Simon Blumenfeld, James Hanley, Emanuel Litvinoff and Frank Tilsley wrote, variously, for the theatre, as well as radio and television. Tilsley, as Worpole points out, was the writer, in 1955, of *The Makepeace Story*, a television serial about a Lancashire cotton family, which could be seen as a precursor of *Coronation Street,* the enduring Northern working class soap. Moreover, as Worpole says, it was on *Coronation Street* that the popular and populist writer of strongly issue- based television drama, Jimmy McGovern, learned his craft, before moving on to *Brookside* and then *The Street*.

The other writer Worpole mentions is Harold Pinter, who, beyond doubt, mined the working class speech of London's East End in his early plays in particular — just as he did the structures of suspense drawn from crime fiction. (Borrowings that a number of British crime writers, myself included, and, more recently still, young British film makers, have sneaked back in spades.) What Worpole neglects to do, however, unless I'm misreading, is direct our attention towards what I regard as one of the most important creative partnerships in British cultural life of the 1960s, that of Tony Garnett and Ken Loach.

The pair first worked together on *Catherine*, a 30-minute television play directed by Loach, with Garnett in an acting role. The play was written by Roger Smith, who was the story editor for *The Wednesday Play*, which ran on the BBC from 1964 until 1970, when it was replaced by the equally adventurous and challenging (well, sometimes) *Play for Today*. Smith brought Garnett in as assistant story editor, and it was in this role that he and Loach worked on the first of their highly controversial television plays, *Up the Junction* (1965).

This piece set the hallmark for so much of their work together. Issue-based social realism — in this case, the issue being backstreet abortion — filmed largely, if not entirely, on location, using a documentary style (in this harking back to the strengths of British cinema production at the time of WW2 and after) and, frequently, employing untrained or little-known actors.

*Up the Junction* was followed a year later by *Cathy Come Home*, perhaps the quintessential Garnett-Loach, and written by Jeremy Sandford, with Garnett now as producer. It's difficult now to imagine the impact that these two pieces had at the time, influencing, as they did, a change in attitudes amongst the public in general. Abortion was legalised in 1967, two years after *Up the Junction* was screened, and *Cathy Come Home*, which was watched by twelve million people, then a quarter of the population, led to the founding of the charity Crisis and serious discussion (if little more) of the problem of homelessness in Parliament.

For the next thirteen years, as producer and director, Garnett and Loach worked on scripts by innovative and radical writers such as Neville Smith, Jim Allen, David Mercer and Barry Hines. In 1969, they made the film *Kes*, adapted for the screen by Hines from his novel, *A Kestrel For a Knave*, published a year earlier.

It's inconceivable to me (while being, of course, unprovable) that any potential or practising writer living in Britain at the time, especially those with an interest in contemporary urban life, would not have been aware of this body of work and, to a greater or lesser degree, influenced by it.

It seeped, sometimes forced its way, into our minds, our bones, our writers' DNA. And for crime writers, embryonic or actual, also, to a lesser degree, part of the Garnett-Loach legacy (though Garnett was only directly involved as an actor), there was *Z-Cars*, a police series which ran from 1962 until 1978, and which, in its early years at least, shared many of the characteristics of the the individual dramas discussed above. It was issue-driven, with a concentration on working-class characters and situations; although, in the beginning especially, many of the scenes were filmed in the studio, there was increasing use of location shooting (with Kirkby, outside

Liverpool, standing in for the fictional Newtown) and a consciously documentary feel.

Created by Troy Kennedy Martin, *Z-Cars* drew from the same pool of writers and directors as *The Wednesday Play* and *Play for Today*. Writers included John McGrath, Allan Prior, John Hopkins (who wrote an astonishing 46 episodes between 1962 and '63) and Alan Plater; McGrath also directed a number of episodes, and, Loach aside, other directors included James MacTaggart, Michael Barry and Ridley Scott.

One other significant writer who contributed scripts to the programme was Ted Lewis, the best-known of whose nine novels is *Jack's Return Home* (1970), which was reissued as *Get Carter*, after Mike Hodges' successful 1971 film starring Michael Caine. With its northern setting (Doncaster or Scunthorpe, opinions differ) and its vivid representation of a scuzzy world of often brutal violence, sexuality and small-scale political corruption, Lewis' novel relates, on one hand, to the world of *Z-Cars*, and, on another, to the tradition of American hard-boiled fiction.

When still at school, Lewis had been introduced to the work of Raymond Chandler by his teacher, the novelist and poet Henry Treece, who read Chandler's work to his English class in a suitable American accent and it is tempting to see in his work a largely successful synthesis of the Chandler-Hammett school of crime fiction with a social realism that references the worlds of British writers such as Sillitoe and film makers such as Ken Loach.

Pivotal, then? Well, maybe.

The problem is that, for all the success of the film on which it was based, Lewis' best-known, we might say best, novel was out of print for a good number of years and his reputation has only slowly grown following his premature death in 1982.

Even so, there's a line, faint but clear, if not a fully-formed family tree, leading from Chandler via the British social realists writers and the *Z-Cars*/Ken Loach axis to where exactly? Rankin? McIlvanney? Me?

William McIlvanney's *Laidlaw* was published in 1977, leading eventually to Ian Rankin's first Rebus novel, *Knots and Crosses*, a decade later, and to *Lonely Hearts*, my own first Resnick novel, published in 1989. All regional; all urban, all chronicling predominantly working class lives.

Let's look first at William McIlvanney. A Scottish novelist whose work deals with issues of masculinity and violence, he followed *Docherty*, set in a mining town during the Depression and winner of the 1975 Whitbread Award for Fiction, with *Laidlaw* (1977), the central character in which is a Glasgow-based detective inspector and which, even more than Ted Lewis' *Jack's Return Home*, successfully welds together the American hard-boiled and the abrasive and hard-edged observation and social concern that characterise McIlvanney's work in general.

Ian Rankin has acknowledged the debt that his Rebus series, set in Edinburgh, owes to McIlvanney, who went on to write about Laidlaw in two more novels, *The Papers of Tony Veitch* (1983) and *Strange Loyalties* (1991). There's a declared indebtedness to Chandler in Rankin's writing also — he is a past winner of a Chandler-Fulbright Award — and he is on record as admiring the work of fellow Scottish writers, Robert Louis Stevenson and James Hogg, whose *Strange Case of Dr. Jekyll and Mr. Hyde* (1886) and *Confessions of a Justified Sinner* (1824) respectively, he claims as major influences. He also, as a student, studied in depth the writing of Muriel Spark for a PhD thesis that went unpublished.

Just when you think you're starting to get it all pinned down, it starts to skid away from you. James Hogg? Muriel Spark?

For myself, my initial forays into crime fiction — reading it, that is — were all American: initially at least, ersatz American, though I doubt if I realised that at the time. And since, as happens with age, although I have difficulty remembering where I left my wallet and keys half an hour ago, my long-term memory is thriving, this section — until the editor gets his hands on it — is on the lengthy side. You have been warned!

So, back to childhood. Early teens, anyway, when most of my spare time reading consisted of westerns, from Allan 'Rocky' Lane comics and Clarence E. Mulford Hopalong Cassidy yarns to weightier stuff like Elliot Arnold's *Blood Brother*. Then, at some point around the age of thirteen or fourteen, a fellow pupil at my Catholic grammar school thrust a well-used copy of a Hank Janson novel into my hands, the book, in all probability, falling open at what were deemed the juiciest pages.

The Janson books, of which there were many, were violent thrillers with both a strident American tone, an American setting and titles like *When Dames Get Tough* and *Smart Girls Don't Talk*; pulp novels in which the promises displayed on the book's jacket — well-endowed blondes wearing blouses several sizes too small and inevitably ripped and torn — were delivered in lubricious and, to my largely innocent mind, barely understandable scenes of sexual clamour. Janson was, in fact, an Englishman — Stephen Daniel Frances — and Hank Janson was both the pen name he wrote under and his central character, a tough reporter-come-detective depicted in silhouette on the corner of every cover.

From Janson I moved on, and a step up, or so I thought — his books were available from the public library, after all — to another Englishman, Peter Cheyney, whose terse and fast-paced pseudo-American thrillers sold phenomenally well in the late 1930s and throughout the '40s. Cheyney had two series characters, Lemmy Caution — an FBI agent working undercover in Britain — and Slim Callaghan, a down-at-heel private detective operating in the seedier parts of London, and whom I always think of as the precursor of Frank Marker, played — gloriously — by Alfred Burke in the television series, *Public Eye,* which ran for ten years from 1965.

Cheyney was born in the East End of London, in Whitechapel, and some of that background shows through in the Callaghan novels, though social realism is far from their creator's mind, and whether Cheyney was aware of the work such writers as Blumenfeld or Westerby, with a similar geographical background to himself, is, as far as I can determine, unknown. The books achieved great popularity in France, a number of them being made into films, most notably by Jean-Luc Godard, whose 1965 futuristic thriller *Alphaville*, is subtitled *Une Étrange Aventure de Lemmy Caution*.

By then I had left Cheyney, Caution and Callaghan behind. But not America. By now easing into the sixth form, I read and re-read the Steinbeck of *Tortilla Flat*, *Cannery Row*, and *Sweet Thursday*, of *The Grapes of Wrath* and *Of Mice and Men*; Nelson Algren. James T. Farrell's Studs Lonigan Trilogy and Erskine Caldwell's *Tobacco Road*. F. Scott Fitzgerald. The less complex novels by Faulkner. And, of course — now we're getting to it — Hemingway. The short stories. *A Farewell to Arms. The Sun Also Rises*. The short stories again. Just about the first piece of fiction writing, other than school assignments, that I tried was an imitation Nick Adams story reset in north London which I made the mistake of showing to my mother — the other reader in the family — who, after a quick perusal, pronounced, "No one's going to want to read anything like that. There's nothing in it." It was a good fifteen years or more before I tried again.

But Hemingway led, by some not so circuitous route, to Chandler. First, the film of *The Big Sleep*, seen at the old Everyman, Hampstead (as opposed to the 'new' posh Everyman), or the National Film Theatre, and thence to the novels, green-backed Penguin paperbacks which I read, at first haphazardly and then in sequence. I remember also sitting on the Backs at Cambridge, behind the colleges and close to the river (no, I was there on a day trip) coming to the final chapters of *The Long Goodbye* with the sad realisation that after that — *Playback* and the unfinished *Poodle Springs* aside — there was nothing more. For some little time afterwards, my friend Jim and myself wandered the streets of suburban Finchley challenging one another to come up with the first line for a new Chandler novel: *He was thirty and needed a shave*, was the best we could manage.

Chandler aside, there were others I read with relish, all, in one way or another, grist to my eventual mill. Dashiell Hammett, though I didn't regard him as highly then as I do now. Ross Macdonald. Ross Thomas. Ed McBain. A little further along, George V. Higgins' superlative *The Friends of Eddie Coyle*. Little or nothing British. No Christie, no Sherlock Holmes. Gerald Kersh I would have heard of, but only through Jules Dassin's 1950 film of his *Night and City*; Curtis, Hamilton, all of the other authors I referred to in my opening paragraph, were not even names. The exception, and it's a meaningful one, would be Graham Greene, whose 'entertainments' such as *A Gun For Sale* and *The Ministry of Fear*, and, crucially, the more 'serious' *Brighton Rock* were to have an influence on my writing that didn't become discernible till much later.

As it happened, my progression as a writer of pulp fiction mirrored the same trajectory as my reading (and that of Elmore Leonard, though I wouldn't have known this at the time) passing from westerns to crime fiction, my initial efforts at the latter — four novels featuring one Scott Mitchell, private eye — struggling and mostly failing to marry hard-boiled American thriller writing and characterisation with an authentic English background. Taking Chandler as a model was, perhaps, the main source of my problem, his style, while suspiciously easy to mimic, in inexperienced hands ending up like poor parody.

Though published, and with covers that would not have looked out of place on one of the Hank Jansons of old, they were, I soon realised, poor work, and, with a few scattered exceptions, it would be a dozen years before I would make any resolute attempt at crime fiction again.

In order to succeed, if succeed I did, it was necessary to slough off the more overbearing trappings of the American tradition I'd been following, retain certain of its features, such as pacing and the use of dialogue both to reveal character and as a way of progressing the action, and embed those within a style and a set of concerns that were rooted in a determinedly English here and now. Here and now for me at that time — 1988/89 — being Nottingham.

By then I'd read — several times — McIlvanney's *Laidlaw*; also — a strong influence on writers from Val McDermid to Henning Mankel — I had read the ten Martin Beck novels by the Swedish pair, Sjöwall and Wahlöö, humane but fiercely political urban police procedurals. Surrounded by his still recognisable city, I was rereading Sillitoe, looking again at those early Lawrence short stories. I'd been reading some recent American crime fiction, too, Walter Mosley, Elmore Leonard, Joseph Wambaugh, Lawrence Block. And when the chance came to devise and write a new drama series for Central Television based on the cases and personal lives of the local probation service, I knew what my models would be. For the documentary style, the social issues and the complexity of characters it was back to *Z-Cars*, updated now with borrowings from the speedily intercut story lines of the American police series, *Hill Street Blues*. The streets were not a million miles from those walked upon by Arthur Seaton — he would have recognised Radford and Forest Fields, felt not out of place in Yates's or on Slab Square — and those were the same streets Charlie Resnick would walk a year or so later in *Lonely Hearts* and the novels that followed, a detective inspector who was as compassionate as Laidlaw, but not as hard, not as haunted, at least not by the same demons. Having, to my eyes, failed lamentably earlier on, if with these books I came close to combining the strengths of the American hard-boiled — and a little of its humour — with the clarity and compassion that marked the British social realists of the 60s and later, novelists and film makers both, I'll not be unhappy. Rather the reverse.

[1] Leslie Fiedler, *Love and Death in the American Novel*, 1960

[2] For a clear and concise introduction to the work of Jim Tully, see *Jim Tully: The Origins of Hard-Boiled Fiction?* on Woody Haut's Blog — http://woodyhaut.blogspot.co.uk/2012/11/jim-tully-origins-of-hardboiled-fiction.html

[3] Peter Messent, *The Crime Fiction Handbook*, 2013

[4] Ken Worpole, *Dockers and Detectives*, second edition, 2008

[5] J.G. Ballard, *Miracles of Life*, 2008

# Marlowe and Me
## *Russel D McLean*

> I was neat, clean, shaved and sober, and I didn't care who knew it. I was everything the well-dressed private detective ought to be. I was calling on four million dollars.
>
> *The Big Sleep*

It began with Humphrey Bogart.

A double bill at the Adam Smith theatre in Kirkcaldy. My dad telling me how these movies were among his favourites. *The Maltese Falcon. The Big Sleep.*

My memory is of the scene in *The Big Sleep* where Lauren Bacall looks Bogie up and down and says, "My, you're a mess, aren't you?" and Bogie, not skipping a beat replies, "I'm not very tall, either. Next time I'll come on stilts, wear a white tie and carry a tennis racket."

That was the moment I'll always associate with Philip Marlowe. Not the words exactly, but the delivery. A flippancy that disguised something else entirely.

Bogie and Marlowe.

They were inseparable in my head. When I did come to read the books, the voice I heard in my mind belonged to Humphrey Bogart. Sure, I saw others do Marlowe and do him well — Dick Powell, Elliot Gould, even James Garner — but none of them got me the way Bogie did. None of their voices affected the way that I read Raymond Chandler.

If you know anything about crime fiction, you'll know that Philip Marlowe, the protagonist of *The Big Sleep*, is the most famous creation of crime writer, Raymond Chandler.

Chandler reinvigorated crime writing and crime readers, even if no one at the time realised quite what he was doing. He took crime fiction and raised it to another level. Removed the predictable patterns of crime, red herring, revelation, giving the crime novel a deeper layer of meaning. Made it political (he tackled the idea of corruption in the LA police department) and personal (*The Long Goodbye* is a deeply affecting novel that gives insight into Chandler as much as it does his fictional creation).

The question is, then, what was so special about Chandler, and in particular, Philip Marlowe? Why has Chandler lasted in mainstream popular culture when so many of his contemporaries, with a few notable exceptions, are these days read only by people who know and admire the mystery of the crime genre?

Why did I come to admire Philip Marlowe over, say, Dashiell Hammett's Sam Spade?

What made him different?

Chandler wasn't interested in clever plots over character and atmosphere. Oh, sure, Chandler's books had intrigue and twists and unexpected danger and a massive number of blows to the head — it's a wonder Marlowe never developed brain damage — but what Chandler was truly interested in was character and atmosphere. If he had a failing, it was that he often wrote a series of scenes that were only loosely connected. The scene, as the man himself said, always mattered more than the story. Critics of Chandler often point towards the story of when *The Big Sleep* was being filmed by Howard Hawkes, and Hawkes suddenly realised he didn't know who killed the Sternwood chauffeur. The legend goes that he telegraphed Chandler to ask who the murderer was. Chandler wired back: "NO IDEA." Chandler merely needed the scene to move the book forward, to put Marlowe in a certain frame of mind so that he could move to the climax.

But Chandler was not writing a mystery story in the traditional sense, and was less interested in the "passage work" that led to the solving of a puzzle. This was a reaction to the kind of criticism that has often been levelled at traditional mystery writers such as Christie *et al.* (Although there is no denying that to write that kind of mystery takes a special kind of talent, too):

> The emotional basis of the standard detective story was and had always been that murder will out and justice will be done. Its technical basis was the relative insignificance of everything except the final denouement. What led up to that was more or less passage work. The denouement would justify everything. The technical basis of the *Black Mask* type of story on the other hand was that the scene outranked the plot, in the sense that a good plot was one which made good scenes. The ideal mystery is one you would read if the end was missing.
> *Trouble is My Business*

So, sure, even as a die-hard Chandlerite, I admit that Chandler sometimes skipped on plot or merely transitioned fast enough from one scene to the next that you only realised they weren't as connected as you might think once you finished the novel. I wouldn't agree with *The Washington Post*'s Patrick Anderson who called Chandler's plots "incoherent and rambling at best". I'd argue that the books stand up for the most part. They connect emotionally, even if they do rely on the reader filling in a few gaps here and there. But Chandler more than made up for this by being one of the few crime writers overtly concerned with voice and atmosphere. He wanted to take the crime novel and use it as an experiment in style. Just because you were writing "disposable" fiction didn't mean you couldn't do it well. And just because you needed to have a guy walk through the door with a gun didn't mean he couldn't do it in style.

It seems obvious in retrospect, but I'd been a Chandler fan long before I read him. As a child, I loved Anthony Horowitz's *Diamond Brothers* novels, books that paid homage to the works of Chandler, Hammett et al. What I loved most about the books were the jokes, the zinging dialogue, the smartness of the characters. These were things that reflected the style of Chandler (albeit in a form more suited to younger readers and without needing to know the source material). Later, what would always stick with me when I discovered Chandler properly was the dialogue and the sheer rhythm of the prose. I'd read other private eye writers. I'd loved Hammett, I'd devoured Erle Stanley Gardner and Lawrence Block, but something about Chandler really sang from the page even upon re-reading. I could lose myself in his writing. And that was something you couldn't say about most writers. And something you still can't. I'm often harsh on crime writing, as much as I love the genre, but it's because I can forgive a stiff plot, but can never forgive stiff writing. Still, too many writers are focussed on plot rather than taking delight in storytelling, in using and abusing language properly. Chandler understood language like no one else before him. And maybe no one else since.

> "You're Marlowe?"
> I nodded.
> "I'm a little disappointed," he said. "I rather expected something with dirty fingernails."
> "Come inside," I said, "And you can be witty sitting down."
> *The High Window*

Philip Marlowe. The Private Investigator's Private Investigator.

Marlowe's the primary reason people still read Chandler. He is the reason people sat up and paid attention to the writer who was born in America, went to school in England with PG Wodehouse and finally returned to the US where he waited for several decades before discovering his ability with the crime story. Before Marlowe — before the pulps — Chandler wanted to be taken seriously as a writer (he still did, even as a crime writer) and wrote some truly awful poetry, which even he referred to as 'sub-grade Georgian' (*Raymond Chandler:*

*A Biography*). Marlowe — and Marlowe's pulp predecessors — gave Chandler the voice he had been looking for all those years.

It took three books before anyone really paid attention to both the author and his creation. Chandler's first publisher, Knopf, insisted for 'prestige' reasons that they publish him in hardback to distinguish him from the rest of the pulp genre who were pumping out novels in cheap paperback editions from publishers such as Ace and Dell. Chandler, Knopf reasoned, was a cut above most of these guys and deserved a smarter audience. But the hardback editions ensured that Chandler failed to reach the audience who would respond to him best; the general reader. Chandler may have had a way with a simile and a raw intelligence that most other crime writers lacked, but he was still writing within the pulp framework he had developed through writing for magazines such as *Black Mask*.

If you read the first three novels, you can see something of Chandler's moods when writing each one of them, given voice through Marlowe. The high points of *The Big Sleep* with Marlowe wisecracking his way through the ins and outs of the case — a reflection of Chandler's own joy at his creation and the fiery love that comes with a first novel — contrast considerably with the more brutal and introspective feel of *The Lady in the Lake*, where Marlowe's more out of control tempers reflect his creators own frustrations, where Marlowe's self-criticism reaches its height mirroring Chandler's own feelings during the writing of the novel. In particular, *The Lady in the Lake* was, according to Tom Hiney's *Raymond Chandler: A Biography*, the only novel that Chandler could not re-read. But it was also the novel that marked a turning point for Chandler's career, becoming his biggest selling US hardback. Why? Knopf had finally allowed a cheap edition of *The Big Sleep* to be published despite their concerns this might somehow damage hardback sales, and even Chandler's reputation. The effect was exactly the opposite. A whole new audience was discovering Chandler, eager to catch up on the further adventures of Philip Marlowe. They snapped up the paperback editions of *The Big Sleep* and *Farewell My Lovely*. The other effect was that more people than ever jumped into the hardback pool for *The Lady in the Lake*. To give you an idea of how the hardbacks were doing at the time, the figures quoted in Hiney's biography of Chandler are 14,000. Still a relatively small figure for a series that would go onto become one of the most well-known within the genre.

So why did the paperback release find such an enthusiastic new audience? It's difficult to say beyond the fact that Chandler's books have a tone and style that clearly resonated with people.

Marlowe is the heart of Chandler's novels, his attitude informing and propelling the books to become more than just cookie-cutter private eye novels. It seems clear, as suggested in the biographies by Hiney and earlier by Frank MacShane, that there is something of Chandler in Marlowe, and this could be what makes people relate to him. Marlowe is a man frustrated by idiocy in others, a man with an innate sense of justice that isn't always equal to the law. He is a man with strong opinions, a man whose moral code is absolute and concrete in his own mind. You could say the same about Chandler. His letters point at a frustration with people he considers foolish, and he clearly has a very strict idea of his own morality, borne out by his education and his own experiences as a soldier.

The author of *A Mysterious Something in the Light*, Tom Williams, talks on his blog about Marlowe's moral code, noting that it is neither British nor American, but is influenced by Chandler's years at Dulwich College. As Williams points out, Marlowe is all about honesty, but is never above lying in the service of a greater truth. The code is one of honour and self-sacrifice, the kind of properties that speak directly to people looking for a hero, who have lost their faith in authority figures. Marlowe embodies all of these qualities, combined with a very human set of flaws. He is not a perfect hero. He is not always right. He is frequently fooled. He is plagued — especially in *The High Window* and *The Lady in the Lake* — with self doubt and a sense of how other people might just be seeing him. His anger and his sarcasm are appealing but often cause more problems than Marlowe might have had otherwise.

People always associate Marlowe with Chandler's famous *The Simple Art of Murder* essay. It is true that what he writes can definitely be related to Marlowe, although Marlowe is never mentioned by name:

> But down these mean streets a man must go who is not himself mean, who is neither tarnished nor afraid. The detective in this kind of story must be such a man. He is the hero, he is everything. He must be a complete man and a common man and yet an unusual man. He must be, to use a rather weathered phrase, a man of honour...
> *Trouble is My Business*

If you read Chandler's early short fiction, this man appears time and again, although not necessarily under the name Marlowe (he comes close with "Mallory", and two of the plots from the *Black Mask* stories were adapted for Marlowe when the detective got his own TV show).

The description — not specific to Marlowe — is of an archetype, a type of hero that Chandler feels is essential to crime fiction. An archetypal hero is not a bad thing. In fact, for popular fiction that survives, it is essential. Archetypal characters are not the same as stereotypes, and there is room for variation among characters with similar essential traits.

Many writers may know the exact date and time of their characters births, the kind of food they prefer, the names of all their brothers and sisters and the first girl they fell in love with at college, but few cut to the heart of their characters, making all the detail seem like mere window dressing to the essential nature of their protagonist. I've already said that Chandler would sacrifice coherency for the sake of the scene, and again with character, he was more interested in what made a good story than in watching the specifics of his character's biography. Marlowe is 33 in *The Big Sleep*, 42 in *The Long Goodbye* (which is set fourteen years later) and Chandler noted in a letter to D.J. Ibberson in 1951 that Marlowe was 38 years old. Marlowe's age fluctuates with Chandler's own moods but his essence remains throughout the novels. The Marlowe we know remains, even if occasionally the details seem fuzzy.

He is a character in the purest sense of the word: we have a strong idea of his strengths and his flaws, and we know him instantly. He presents himself to us fully and honestly. We see Marlowe as a person, not a set of statistics of deliberately assigned traits.

> Guns never scare me... they are just a fast curtain to a bad second act.
> *Playback*

Marlowe has been with us in one form or another long after Chandler's death. People keep returning to him, looking to him as a touchstone for the private eye genre. We've had updates of the character, most notably Elliot Gould's 1970's Marlowe in *The Long Goodbye*, and we've seen his influence dominate films and screenplays to the present day, with generations of novelists and screenwriter cranking up the kind of wisecracks that Marlowe was famous for; two recent examples being *The Big Lebowski* and *Kiss, Kiss, Bang, Bang,* the latter in particular wearing its Chandlerian influence on its sleeve, right down to naming each act after a Chandler novel. The Marlowe novels themselves remain bestsellers, and are often taught at universities. Modern hardboiled crime novelists are frequently compared by critics to Chandler. After Chandler's death, Robert B. Parker finished the final Marlowe novel, *Poodle Springs* and wrote an original Marlowe of his own. In 2013, the crime writer Benjamin

Black (a pseudonym for John Banville) will write a new Marlowe novel approved by the Chandler estate.

But no ersatz Marlowe, or Marlowe imitator, will ever be able to replicate the one written by Chandler, although some may be able to entertain us in their own fashion. Chandler and Marlowe are inseparable.

Tom Williams writes in his introduction to *A Mysterious Something in the Light* that, "[Chandler] hoped that he would eventually be able to move beyond his most famous creation... and one day be able to forget mystery stories altogether," but this was something he would rarely admit in public. Perhaps because in part he did love the genre, but also, "with each apparently futile attempt to write something other than a crime novel he managed to expand the boundaries of what it was possible to achieve within the genre and, in doing so, turned it into an art.". Chandler needed Marlowe to say what he needed to say, and Marlowe needed Chandler to give him voice.

Marlowe is a character who appeals from generation to generation. He is fully formed in his creator's mind and leaps onto the page as a completely relatable and understandable psychology. He is a flawed archetype who speaks to qualities that we admire and sympathise with. He is a product of his time whose values are ultimately timeless and human, whose regrets are our own, whose strengths can also be his weakness.

He is a character who endures, a character who inspires, one of the few truly immortal series characters of crime fiction who refuses to wither with age, who still affects readers old and new in the same way he did when he first appeared. Philip Marlowe endures. And something in that is comforting to me. He may be forever associated with the '40s and '50s, but he is a character who appeals to readers across the decades, whose voice and attitude ring true even more than half a century after his first appearance.

# Further Reading:

*Raymond Chandler:* Frank MacShane
*Raymond Chandler: A Biography:* Tom Hiney
*A Mysterious Something in the Light:* Tom Williams
*Chandler Speaking*: collected by Frank MacShane

And of course:
The novels of Raymond Chandler

# What You Don't Know about Nottingham
## Fact and Fiction in a Series of Political Crime Novels
*David Belbin*

My fascination with politics began in my mid-teens, stoked by the McGovern/Nixon election in the US. In the UK Labour was in power and right wing, so I joined the Young Liberals, all of whom (in Pendle, at least) seemed to be anarchists. Only for a year, but I got to know a bunch of Liberal councillors (one now in the Lords) and helped out in various ways. Later my mother would join the same party and become mayor, but that's another story.

At university, student politics seemed infantile, so I didn't get involved. Then, shortly after graduating, I started to write a novel about the aftermath of a nuclear war, the research for which led me to join Notts for Nuclear Disarmament. This proved to be the gateway drug for a ten year addiction to political activism. Michael Foot had just become Labour's leader and Thatcher needed opposing. Within a few months, I was a NUPE branch chair, a Labour General Committee member and a governor of several schools. I was a council candidate (for the area where I now live) and branch chairman of the Robin Hood ward, amongst other dubious honours.

Ten years later, I left, partly because of Labour's drift to the right, largely because I had just had my first novel published. I was concerned that my freedom of expression might be hampered by membership of a political party. But my interest remained, and I did keep in close touch with both local and national politics. Several of my friends — and one or two of my enemies — would become

Members of Parliament. And the political junky habit kept surfacing in my fiction. My first novel, *The Foggiest*, featured scenes set in the House of Commons. My twelve novel sequence about young police officers, *The Beat*, published between 1993 and 2000 had a recurring character who was a cunning Tory minister.

These were novels for Young Adults, teenagers. I became aware that, if I wanted to write more directly about how the political process affects people's lives, I needed to write novels for adults. Therefore, in 1996, when it was clear that New Labour were going to win the next General Election, I visited the Commons as a guest of my MP, John Heppell, Labour MP for Nottingham East, and began research for the novel that was to become *Bone and Cane*. John agreed to give me an unpaid, part-time job as a parliamentary researcher. At this stage, my model, insofar as I had one, was the television series *Bill Brand*, written by Trevor Griffiths and broadcast in 1976, about an idealistic young Labour MP, played by Jack Shepherd.

I visited the Commons again a month after the election, but not as a researcher. Labour's then chief whip, the late Donald Dewar, over-ruled my appointment on the grounds that, as a professional writer, I might leak stories to *Private Eye* and the like. He was wrong, but he did me a favour. For, in trying to begin the novel that I wanted to write, I quickly realised that it's hard to write about a historical period until it's over. Griffiths, for instance, wrote *Bill Brand* at the end of the Wilson era, and I would not be able to start in earnest until Tony Blair was well into his final term.

I wrote a lot of crime novels in the 90's and wanted to explore the limits of the genre. But, after *The Beat* novels, I wasn't interested in writing about the police again. I'd been the first author to write a series about young police officers, which gave me a new angle. After that I didn't (still don't) think there were any new angles left. I did give my fictional MP, Sarah Bone, a brief period as a police officer — her joining the police was what split her up with the other protagonist. He's a school teacher, Nick Cane, who grows cannabis in the caves beneath his Nottingham flat and goes to prison for five years.

At the start of *Bone and Cane*, Nick's released and the 1997 General Election is called. Immediately Nick gets mixed up with a double murderer. Ed Clark has just got out on appeal after a campaign run by Sarah, who was Nick's university girlfriend. While Nick was in prison, Sarah won a by-election to become a New Labour MP, for a fictional Nottingham seat, Nottingham West. A seat with this name used to exist (I lived in it) but was abolished by boundary changes in the 1980s. The next, now delayed set of boundary changes is likely to restore it. In my fictional version, West is normally a safe Conservative seat, so is likely to return to the Tories at the General Election. *Bone and Cane* has two mysteries — who committed the two murders, and who betrayed Nick to the police. But the biggest source of suspense in the novel is whether Sarah will be re-elected, and the lengths to which she will go to achieve that aim.

The original title of the novel, before I was persuaded (for commercial reasons) to name it after the protagonists, was *Previous Convictions*. This sums up the theme, not just of this novel, but of the sequence as a whole. Can Nick build a worthwhile life despite his prison record, which he must always declare to employers? And how can Sarah reconcile the political convictions that brought her into politics in the first place with the reality of being in government?

Sarah does get re-elected, by a narrow majority. And Tony Blair offers her a job in the government. Not in the cabinet, but as a junior minister in the Home Office. For prisons. This means that the very last person she should have a relationship with is somebody who has just been released from one. That the two protagonists still have strong feelings for each other but cannot get back together until Sarah ceases to be an MP is one of the major tropes of the sequence.

We've all seen fictional representations of government, in satires from *Yes, Minister* to *The Thick Of It*. There are numerous dramas populated by exaggerated characters who rarely bear much resemblance to the government of the time that they are portraying. I didn't want to work that way. I wanted to write a realistic, credible account of both Nottingham and New Labour. Not documentary. Not faction, where real events are portrayed in a way that combines journalism and creative writing, a form in which characters can be composited but the author owes the audience accuracy to verifiable events.

The first novel took place during an election campaign, when Parliament wasn't sitting. Tony Blair and Gordon Brown make brief appearances, on the end of a phone. There may be an ethical issue here, which I'll come to, but, legally, I appeared to be on safe ground. Prime Ministers don't sue: it's beneath their dignity. Donald Dewar, the Chief Whip, also appears, partly because he's useful in the plot, and partly as an acknowledgement that he'd had a role in the genesis of the novel. He, too, can't sue, because he died in 2000. Ethically, I didn't see a problem in portraying him. Literature has a long tradition of fictionalising historical figures. Novels by David Peace and Jake Arnott, amongst others, feature famous people from the 60s and 70s.

But what about the other living people I needed to appear in the story that I was going to tell? There were two immediate issues. The real prisons minister in the first New Labour administration was a woman, Joyce Quin, who is now in the House of Lords. She can be seen in the famous *Blair's Babes* photo. Should I contact Baroness Quin of Gateshead, for background? I decided not to. I didn't want her experience to colour Sarah's fictional experience, which needed to be whatever was necessary to both the plot of this novel and the sequence as a whole. Sarah brought her own agenda to the job, particularly a concern about prisoners with HIV, that has no connection to Baroness Quin's time as prisons minister.

Then there was Quin's boss. The Home Secretary in 1997-8 was Jack Straw. In an early draft of the beginning of the novel, I included him as a named character. Straw is an interesting New Labour figure who I could probably have gained access to. Fictionalising him, however, was fraught with problems, both ethical and creative. Not just in this novel, but further down the line. For instance, the third novel, nearly ready at the time of writing, makes mention of the extradition of General Pinochet, with which Straw was indelibly involved.

I decided to rewrite the Straw character as *The Home Secretary*. He is not fictionalised, but nor is he characterised. This is a compromise, but doesn't seem to have interfered with readers' ability to suspend their disbelief and enjoy the novel. There was a further dilemma. During the timespan of *What You Don't Know*, there was a well documented incident concerning Straw's son that related directly to the theme of my novel. This was the trickiest thing to deal with, and I changed my mind about how to handle it several times — twice after the manuscript had been edited. Read page 85 of the published novel if you want to find out what I did in the end.

While I am writing historically about New Labour, I am also writing a history of Nottingham, where I have lived since 1977. I've written about the city many times before: in the 1998 novel *Love Lessons*, in a 2011 novel about asylum seekers and allotments, *Secret Gardens* and in *The Beat*. *Love Lessons* is set in 1995, but the others have no specific time scale. The final *Beat* novel was written in 1999 and published in 2000. It uses the construction of the tram lines that year as part of a storyline. But the full sequence, while written over seven years, occupies just two years, the probationary period of a police officer.

*What You Don't Know* has two major plot-lines which, unsurprisingly, will turn out to be linked. One of them came from my final years as a school-teacher. In the early 90's, I was drawn into the care set-up of a girl in my tutor group who was living at a girls' hostel in a rather shabby, but formerly grand part of Nottingham called Alexandra Park, on the edge of Nottingham's most under-privileged area, the St Ann's estate.

Unusually, this young woman wanted to go on and take A-levels. I was shocked to discover that, in the memory of the people I spoke to at Social Services, this had never happened before. My Head of Year and I went to some trouble to set up a meeting at the hostel where she lived. While we were involved in this I discovered a statistic that I still find hard to take in. 60% of the girls in care in Nottingham end up in prostitution.

Sixty per cent. While I was writing *What You Don't Know*, I attended an event at Nottingham Arena featuring Ed Miliband, who had just become leader of the Labour Party. I found myself sat next to someone who worked in child protection. I asked her about this sixty per cent figure and whether it still held true. *No*, she said. *It's more than that now*. This trap, and how a young girl might escape it, would become crucial in my story. Only after it was published, when I was writing the afterword to one of the new digital editions of my *The Beat* novels, *Dead White Male*, did I remember that I'd used a similar experience for a minor character in that novel, too.[1]

The *Bone and Cane* sequence had to begin in 1997, because of the General Election. Later that year, there was a Nottingham news story that begged to be turned into a novel. The late 90's saw the beginning of an epidemic in the use of crack cocaine, a very powerful, hugely addictive, smokeable form of cocaine. A charity set up a project, the Crack Action Team, that was backed by the city and county council. One local MP was closely involved in the project. All three local MPs backed it. Unbeknownst to any of them, the person they employed to run the team, Dave Francis, used the CAT as a front to become the biggest drugs dealer in the city.

I first heard about the case in a *World In Action* documentary that aired while Francis was still in post. *The*

*Guardian* journalist Nick Davies wrote extensively about the affair in his book *Dark Heart*. Carl Felstrom, in his book, *Hoods*, a history of Nottingham crime over the last two decades, interviews Francis and brings the story up to date. Both are credited in the acknowledgements of the second *Bone & Cane* novel.

Since 2002, I've had a part time job as a senior lecturer at Nottingham Trent University, teaching Creative Writing and English Literature. A piece of creative writing can stand as a piece of research in the academic sense, so I applied for and was granted research leave to work on the novel. The majority of the first draft would be written during my sabbatical. In applying for that leave, though, I had to fill in a form that asked me to consider the ethical issues affecting my research. This question doesn't often cause problems for literary researchers. In my case, however, it immediately raised a pressing issue. For my story was largely inspired by the Crack Action Team debacle and the person at the centre of it had just been released from prison.

Should I talk to a convicted criminal? Should I put him in the novel at all? The issue wasn't so much that Dave Francis could sue for defamation — he had been found guilty of the events that that I wanted to write about, after all — so much as that I didn't want to be my novel to be hampered by knowing the real man. I had no intention of contributing to a mythology that glorifies criminals, but that wasn't my main concern. The biggest issue in fictionalising the CAT fiasco was that the real story overshadowed anything that I could possibly make up. While conducting research interviews, I found out a lot about Francis, but he was not my subject. He was a symptom of the disease that I wanted to write about: the war on drugs.

A novel is an imaginative endeavour, and every novelist approaches their work differently. I plan, but I do not plan meticulously, and I tend never to look at my plan as I am writing. I developed my research methodology while working on *The Beat* series, where I took care to make certain legal and police procedures accurate, but soon learned that too much research beforehand could hamper my ability to tell a good story. Much of the pre-novel research was wasted, anyway, because most of the questions I needed to ask only become clear once I had started writing. One of my most useful contacts is a current Labour MP who answers email promptly so that, if I make up something in the morning that turns out to be impossible, I can often correct it by the afternoon.

Early in the first draft, I spoke to the MP most closely involved with Dave Francis, Alan Simpson, who I've known for more than thirty years. He was, until the last election, the MP for Nottingham South. I wanted a left-wing MP's perspective on the early days of the Blair administration. Alan talked at length about the Single Parent Benefits cut that caused the first major rebellion of the New Labour administration, and I chose to use this in the early part of the novel. Then we talked about Dave Francis, how charismatic he was, the methods he used to pull the wool over people's eyes and how, at first, the stories about him seemed to be malicious, racially motivated. Later, when I gave him a proof copy of the novel, Alan told me that he regarded the case as the most embarrassing episode of his seventeen years as an MP.

As I recall, it was after this conversation that I made the crucial creative decision that was to determine the course of the novel. Instead of writing about the real CAT affair, a story so wide ranging and preposterous that it would stretch any reader's credulity, I decided to apply a lesson that I'd learnt from the novels of my near neighbour and close friend Stanley Middleton, who had died the year before: that often the way to get at the truth of a situation is to write not about the event itself, but the aftermath.

I created a fictional successor to the Crack Action Team, a small scale rehabilitation project for young people called *The Power Project*. Sarah — as the one local

MP not tarred by association with the CAT, was invited onto the board. Nick, as a former teacher with drug experience, was uniquely qualified to work for them. The project would be under suspicion and close scrutiny from the start. Naturally, its boss, a religious figure called Kingston Bell, is soon suspected of corruption, even though he has been chosen precisely because he appears to be squeaky clean.

The story has twists and turn and characters that aren't relevant to this particular discussion. Sex and drugs and family secrets play their part. I used prolepsis to hook the reader from the start, trailing a murder that will not take place until the closing chapters. I also added a third point of view to that of the two series protagonists, using the second person, so that it isn't initially apparent who this narrator is: another mystery.

*What You Don't Know* had the best reception of my novels to date (though not, so far, the sales figures to match: its publisher was on the verge of going under). But what do I know as a result of completing it? Part of the reason I write novels is to explain the world to myself, to ask questions I don't know the answer to. The finished novel is, in itself, my response to those questions. Often I'm left with more questions, ones that may lead to further novels. But not answers, as such. The novel displays an implicit attitude about the uselessness of the 'war on drugs', which is at odds with that of recent governments and will put off some crime readers. My fiction, whether it's marketed for Young Adults or grown-ups, always had a campaigning element, and an educational one, but I want the reader to work out their own moral — or lack of one — rather than directly propagandising. Like any half decent writer, I often play the devil's advocate and give him the best lines. The use of real people and actual events raises the stakes, certainly. Where does a writer draw the line between fact and fiction? Good question. Andy Croft writes, in his verse novel, *1948*:

*What is art if not the tension/*
*Between what's true and what's invention.*

Good answer.

---

[1] The week after *What You Don't Know* was published, a woman called out my name in the queue at the city centre Waitrose. It was twenty years since she'd left school, but I recognised her at once. She did complete her A levels, had a good job and seemed content with her life. Turned out she lives less than half a mile from me.

# Waking the Silent Suspect
## *Hilary Spiers*

*A busy police headquarters. People on phones, others rushing to and fro. The occasional old timer parked on some else's desk eating a bacon butty, having a chinwag. Gilda, the hatchet-faced female boss, leans over the end of the desk of DS Mike Stanforth, a hard-nosed detective passed over for promotion.*

**Gilda**  What you got then, Mark? Come on, I'm a busy and ruthless woman angling for Police Commissioner by the end of the series.

**Mike**  SD after an RTA. DOA. Thing is, victim was under obbo. He'd done time. He was a nark. And the name's Mike. Guv.

**Gilda**  I know it's Mike. I said 'Mark' to fool the other officers that we don't know each other as intimately as we obviously do. That's why I'm studiously avoiding looking at you, while wearing inappropriately low cut tops. What's the score?

**Mike**  Scumbags one, police nil. I suppose you're here to impose some arbitrary deadline to solve the crime within a ridiculously short timeframe?

**Gilda**  Just racheting up the tension, Mike. How's the new boy Gideon fitting in?

**Mike**  What, the fast-track smart-arse you landed me with after my partner was so tragically shot? Him with a poncy degree and a lot to learn, who occasionally spots something I've missed?

**Gilda**  Leave it. Don't go there, Mike. You know why you got passed over for promotion. We both know. I warned you. Don't say I didn't. Walk with me.

*They start walking down interminable corridors.*
*Colleagues hurry past repeatedly.*

**Mike**  What's this in aid of?

**Gilda**  One, it gives a greater sense of urgency than an interview in my office. That's usually reserved for occasions when I close the blinds, and then everyone knows we're shagging. Two, it gives some disaffected officer or passing crim the opportunity to earwig and engineer a plot complication. And three, it makes me look important and I can ask questions about your team as if I've never seen any of them before or been in charge of an investigation myself before I got promoted over your head because I'm female and I've got a stunning chest. (*A woman hurries past them*) Who's that?

**Mike**  Jobbing actress too unattractive to deserve a name who moans a lot. Gets me my tea and bacon butties. She's just going through hours of CCTV footage, sighing heavily, waiting for me to amble over and say, 'Wait a minute! What's that? Run that back.'

**Gilda**  You want to watch it, Mike.

**Mike**  I do! That's how I —

**Gilda**  No, I meant the bacon butties. All that cholesterol — you're prime heart attack fodder.

**Mike**  No worries, Guv. I only ever get to take one bite before there's a breakthrough and I have to grab my signature raincoat and dash out. I never eat properly or change my shirt.

**Gilda**  (*A suspicious looking colleague passes*) And him?

**Mike**  Oh, disaffected DI with a shady past that somehow got missed by police checks who's in deep with some Mr Big he owes money to. He may also have a father with an undisclosed criminal record. Almost certainly accessing confidential files without authorisation. If not porn.

**Gilda**  Any leads? Time's running out, Mike. I've got the old man on my back. Don't let me down. We go back a long way. If life hands you lemons, make lemonade. Come on, Mike, cut in before we go into cliché overload –

**Mike**  I've just sent the two DIs with interchangeable names and fairly unremarkable features — although one is slightly more attractive and might release a record in a year or two — to arrest the dead man's wife and take her down for faking the RTA.

**Gilda**  Excellent. Don't tell me that grieving widow malarkey was just an act?

**Mike**  'Course. The minute I clapped eyes on her, it was obvious she was the guilty party.

**Gilda**  How's that?

**Mike**  She went on dead-heading her roses and barely being civil to us when we arrived to inform her of her husband's demise. Far too much of a looker to just have a bit part as a dead man's wife. That, and she was wearing a blouse unbuttoned even lower than yours.

**Gilda**  The slag! Good work, Mike. I'll see you at the usual smoke-filled pub this evening where we can exchange hot looks while you gaze wistfully at my cleavage. Carry on.

**Curtain**

# Acknowledgements

**Alan Dent**'s "One Day in Whitehaven" appeared on www.pennilesspress.co.uk in July 2010

**Melanie McGrath**'s "Riders on the Storm" first appeared in *The Guardian* on Saturday 13 February 1999

**Jon McGregor**'s article on coroner's courts first appeared in *The Guardian* on Saturday 23 January 2010

**Rod Madocks** would like to thank Christopher Mitchell and Warwickshire and West Mercia Police for assistance concerning photographs for his article

**Hilary Spiers**' "Waking the Silent Suspect" first appeared in *Species,* Laundrette Publications, Nottingham Trent University

**Cathi Unsworth**'s article "The Dark Eyes of London" was first presented as a talk for Gresham College at The Museum of London on Monday 25 June 2012 as part of the Literary London Crime series


All other articles and essays appear here for the first time. Copyright rests with the contributors.

# Selected Five Leaves Books by Contributors to Crime

**Paul Barker** is the editor of *Arts in Society*, a set of essays that first appeared in *New Society*.

**David Belbin**'s most recent books for Five Leaves are *Student* — a "new adult" book and *Secret Gardens*, a novel about refugee children for young adults.

**John Stuart Clark**'s travel book *After the Gold Rush: a bicycle journey through American history* is available now in an ebook edition.

**Michael Eaton** contributed the story "No Smoke" to the crime fiction collection *City of Crime*.

**John Harvey**'s young adult fiction novel *Nick's Blues* and his novella *Trouble in Mind* are available in print and ebook editions.

**John Lucas** has written and edited several books for Five Leaves, his latest being *A Brief History of Whistling* (with Allan Chatburn).

**Jon McGregor**'s stories appeared in the collections *Sunday Night and Monday Morning* and *The Sea of Azov*.

**Russel D. Mclean**'s Dundee crime novels are all published by Five Leaves. The latest is *Father Confessor*.

**Rod Madocks**' second book with Five Leaves, a collection of short stories, *Ship of Fools: stories from the mental health front line* is now available. His first novel, *No Way To Say Goodbye*, was shortlisted for the ITV/Crime Thriller Awards.

**Deirdre O'Byrne** teaches Irish and English literature at Loughborough University and is Chair of Nottingham Irish Studies Group www.nottinghamisg.org.uk. She is also a storyteller and a teacher of the Irish language. Her essays on Eavan Boland and Marge Piercy, appeared in *Maps* and *Utopia*.

**Peter Mortimer**'s latest book is *Made in Nottingham: a writer's return*.

**Danuta Reah**'s crime novella *Not Safe* draws on her experience of working with refugees in Sheffield.

**Damien Seaman**'s first crime novel is *The Killing of Emma Gross*.

**Cathi Unsworth** contributes a chapter on Lynne Reid Banks' *The L-Shaped Room* to *London Fictions*.

# Contributors

From 1996 to 1999, **Paul Barker** wrote a weekly *New Statesman* column about places, under the title 'Observations'. This column appeared on 1 May 1988. Long time editor of *New Society* and now a senior research fellow of the Young Foundation, Paul Barker's recent books include *Arts in Society* (revised edition, Five Leaves, 2006), *The Freedoms of Suburbia* (Francis Lincoln, 2009) and *Hebden Bridge: a sense of belonging* (Francis Lincoln, 2012). In 2013, he published a crime novel, *A Crooked Smile* (as an e-book). His Observation columns on Leeds and New Lanark were reprinted in *Maps* and *Utopia*.

**David Belbin** first made his name as a gritty and worldly writer of books for young adults, featuring issues such as race, loss of virginity, homosexuality and bullying, within a strong and honest narrative. His 2011 adult crime book *Bone and Cane* was the best selling novel across Amazon for three weeks. The follow-up book, *What you Don't Know*, was published in January 2012. His Five Leaves novel *The Pretender* has been translated into several languages.

**John Stuart Clark** is a sometime travel writer, comics commentator and the wordsmith within political cartoonist and comics creator, **Brick**. Currently completing his investigation into *Leonardo's Bicycle* and co-editing graphic compendiums about WWI, refugees and mental distress, he is also a part-time forest ranger. His most recent book is *Depresso: or how I learnt to stop worrying and embrace being bonkers*.

**Alan Dent** conducts a one-man guerilla campaign against the British literary mainstream at Penniless Press. His anthology of contemporary French counter-cultural poetry, *When the Metro is Free* and his translation of Francis Combes' major work *Common Cause* are both published by Smokestack.

**Michael Eaton** has written drama-documentaries including *Shoot To Kill, Why Lockerbie?* and *Shipman* for television; *The Conflict Is Over* and *Washington 9/11* for radio, and *The Families of Lockerbie* for theatre. He is contributing to the perpetuation of the myth of Charlie Peace with a new play to be produced at Nottingham Playhouse in the autumn of 2013.

**Ann Featherstone** is an internationally-published writer, with translations of her books in both French and Italian. She writes historical novels which are set in the entertainment world of the 19th century, and specialises in that area of theatre-history in her day job, teaching undergraduates at the University of Manchester. Her latest novel is *The Newgate Jig*.

Ever since he was awarded the CWA Cartier Diamond Dagger for Sustained Excellence in Crime Writing in 2007, **John Harvey** has been trying, unsuccessfully, to shrug off the implication that everything, henceforth, is downhill. No matter how many mental push-ups, how many twelve mile rambles across the South Downs, the label "veteran crime writer" clings to him like a shroud. His latest effort to disprove the onset of senility is the 12th (and final) Resnick novel, *Darkness, Darkness*, to be published by William Heinemann in May, 2014.

**John Lucas** is the publisher at Shoestring Press and a jazz musician. He was Professor of English at Loughborough and then Nottingham Trent University. His many books include *Next Year Will Be Better: a memoir of England in the 1950s*. With Basil Haynes, he is currently writing a book on cricketing rebels.

**Melanie McGrath** writes for the *Guardian* and other newspapers. Her last two books were crime fiction, *White Heat* and *The Boy in the Snow*, both set in the Arctic. Her other books include *Silvertown: an East End Family Memoir* and *Motel Nirvana*, on the New Age movement.

**John McGregor** is the author of three novels and one collection of short stories, his most recent book. Two of his novels have been longlisted for the Booker Prize. His first, *If Nobody Speaks of Remarkable Things* won the Betty Trask and Somerset Maugham Prize and his collection of short stories, *This Isn't the Sort of Thing That Happens to Someone Like You,* won the East Midlands Book Award.

**Russel D. McLean** is the author of three novels *The Good Son, The Lost Sister* and *Father Confessor*. His debut, *The Good Son*, was shortlisted for a Shamus Award by the Private Eye Writers of America. He has worked as a bookseller for over ten years and is currently writing his fourth novel.

**Peter Mortimer** has just clocked up forty years as editor of Iron Press, of Cullercoats in the North East. He is a playwright and artistic director of Cloud Nine theatre group. His best known book is *Broke Through Britain*. His Five Leaves title, *Camp Shatila*, described how he set up a children's theatre in Shatila Palestinian refugee camp, which then came on tour to the North East.

**Danuta Reah** also writes under the name Carla Banks. She is the author of several novels of psychological suspense and academic books used as resources for the study of language. She is the past Chair of the Crime Writers' Association and is currently working on a novel based on her Polish roots.

**Damien Seaman**'s first crime novel, *The Killing of Emma Gross* is available as an ebook from Blasted Heath and in a re-edited print version from Five Leaves. The book is based on a true, unsolved crime in Weimar Germany. Damien used to live in Berlin, and now lives in Birmigham. He contributes to many crime websites and ezines.

**Hilary Spiers**' short story collection, *The Hour Glass,* is published by Pewter Rose Press and her work has featured in anthologies, on the radio and on stage at the Hampstead Theatre and Stamford Theatre. She wrote the book for the opera The Yellow Dress (Tête à Tête Festival, Riverside Studios, August 2012) and has just completed her second novel, Hester & Harriet. She is in the second year of an MA in Creative Writing at Nottingham Trent University.

**Cathi Unsworth** began her writing career as a journalist on the music weekly, *Sounds* and she has contributed to many other music and cultural journals including *Mojo* and *Uncut*. She edited the major anthology *London Noir* and her own latest novel is *Weirdo*, a tale of teenage trauma and female transgression set in Norfolk.

Mike Marqusee  Let's Talk Utopia
Ken Worpole  Tolstoy in Essex
Gillian Darley  Moravian Graveyards
John Payne  The Putney Debates
William Morris  A Factory As It Might Be
Colin Ward  The Factory We Never Had
Mandy Vere  News from Nowhere Bookshop
John Lucas  In New Zealand
Chris Moss  In Paraguay
Deirdre O'Byrne  Woman on the Edge of Time
Paul Barker  New Lanark
Dennis Hardy  Catching a Bus to Paradise
Paul Summers  The Shadow of Chimneys
Pippa Hennessy  Keeping It in the Family
Leon Rosselson  Singing About William Morris
David Rosenberg  Freedom Without Territory
J. David Simons  Kibbutz: the Golden Age
Will Buckingham  The Trouble with Happiness
Andy Rigby  Communes Revisited
Mike Pentelow and Peter Arkell  Down the Pub
Jeff Cloves  Stroud and Whiteway
Ian Clayton  My Grandmother's Kitchen
Peter Preston  Dreaming London
Haywire Mac  The Big Rock Candy Mountain

# UTOPIA

2012
241 pages
978-1-907869-50-1
**£9.99**

A quirky compendium of essays on maps, places and people, many by leading writers, including Iain Sinclair and *The Guardian*'s David McKie and Chris Arnot, as well as writers from the *London Review of Books*, academic journals, a journalist from the BBC World Service and several biographers.

**Iain Sinclair** Walking Through Liverpool
**Chris Arnot** Lost Cricket Grounds of England
**David Belbin** Grahame Green in Nottingham
**Ross Bradshaw & Ian Parks** The Land of Green Ginger
**Andy Croft** Reading Poetry in Siberia
**Richard Dennis** Mapping Gissing's Novels
**Gillian Darley** Ian Nairn and Jack Kerouac: On the Road
**Roberta Dewa** Wilford: an English Village in the 1950s
**John Lucas** Uprisings in the South West
**David McKie** The Mapping of Surnames
**Deirdre O'Byrne** The Famine Roads of Ireland
**John Payne** Death on the Border: Walter Benjamin
**Mark Patterson** A Short Walk up Dere Street
**Andrew Whitehead** Beyond Boundary Passage: London Fiction
**Sara Jane Palmer** A Walk to Tafraoute
**Paul Barker** The Other Britain: Leeds
**Robert Macfarlane** The Guga Men

"a curious rattle-bag of writing" *Guardian*

"reading [Maps] is akin to peeling back layers, deciphering faded contours and, occasionally, redrawing an entire geography. If travel journalism wants to adapt to the recession, here's a direction it might follow."
*Time Out*

# MAPS

2011
159 pages
978-1-907869-24-2
£7.99

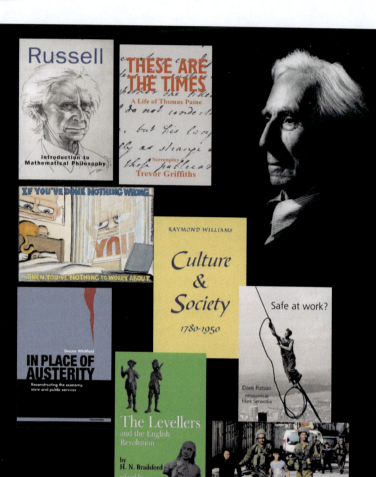